Applied Yogic Science

Applied Yogic Science

(Learning and Teaching)

Kamakhya Kumar
Sudhanshu Verma

SHIPRA

₹ 395
ISBN: 978-93-91978-56-3

2025
First Published in India

Applied Yogic Science
(Learning and Teaching)

Published by:
SHIPRA PUBLICATIONS
LG 18-19, Pankaj Central Market
I.P. Ext., Patparganj, Delhi 110092, India
+91 11 47322068; 96500 28065, 9810522367
info@shiprapublication.com
www.shiprapublication.com

Dedicated to:

Paramhamsa Swami Niranjanananda Saraswati
Founder, Bihar Yoga Bharati

Contents

Introduction

Yoga is an applied science. The information available in the world of knowledge is useless if it is not applicable. Fortunately, Yogic science has deep roots in philosophy and the branches are highly grown into the sky of application. Every aspect of Yoga is useful for the mankind. Whether it is of any form, any style, any tradition or any step of any branch, the term used into Yogic world justifies itself.

Even people having information of these branches don't know how to apply them in the daily life. Some of the students come and ask to the teachers please leave these philosophical topics let us discuss on the applicable aspects. Let me know how to reduce the body weight or how to relax the mind. They don't understand that practice of Yoga is not for health purpose only. There are lot of benefits of other branches of Yoga as well if we know the application of them.

Basically, people coming to the Yoga field feels that there are some physical postures, few breathing techniques and a short of meditation and that I know well. But the thing is the newcomers have seen only few glimpses of this vast knowledge, like having few drops of an ocean. As the postures (Asana) or breathing techniques (Pranayama) are only a few steps of Hatha Yoga, whereas many branches of Yoga like: Bhakti Yoga, Gyan Yoga, Karma Yoga, Raja Yoga etc are untouched to them.

The present volume will not only radiate the application of different practices of different paths of Yoga but it will guide the readers how to make the theories more applicable and more useful. Particularly the new generation coming to the field of Yoga with a purpose of making their career in this field and wish to learn Yoga in a complete manner will definitely get the complete solution in their life.

Dr Kamakhya Kumar
Dr Sudhanshu Verma

1
Concept of Applied Yoga and its Objectives

Introduction to Yoga

Over the years, yoga has gained popularity as a practical system of physical development and improvement of mental and emotional capabilities. When yoga is applied for health promotion in disease states, it is termed as applied yoga. In this type of yoga, lifestyle modification tools of classical yoga are implemented. This paper highlights the concept of applied yoga in health promotion and disease management. Traditional concepts of yoga and its practical implementation are explored, elucidating the role of yoga in health. Whether we realise its importance or not, yoga will continue to be a ray of light for health promotion, well-being, and psychological issues for many years to come. The implementation of yogic principles will continue to work wonders in health as long as the individual reaps the benefits by applying them sincerely.

The discipline of yoga is an ancient science that has evolved over thousands of years. It has been described and defined in several texts such as the *Upanishads*, the *Bhagavad Gita*, and the Yoga Sutras of Patanjali. Yoga seeks to realize truths about our inner nature by applying the concepts of its philosophy in the practical realm through its physical and mental practices. The term 'yoga' is derived from two root words *'Yujir'* and *'Yuj'* which mean 'to join or unite', a term that is used in the physics of sound. The ancient wisdom of India speaks of two inner sounds, the first sound being the sound of life and the second sound being the sound of consciousness. When the two sounds unite, one experiences yoga in its ultimate form, the union of the individual self with the universal self. Due to its benefits in health, it is now a part of integrative medicine systems and is recognized as integrative oncology, integrative psychiatry, and integrative cardiology.

Definition and Origin of Yoga

There are three schools of yoga: Mantra Yoga, Laya Yoga, and Raja Yoga, out of the 520 schools, of which Patanjali Yoga is one. According to the Indian Institute of Applied Yoga, *Mandya*, "Yoga is a scientific way to exert pressure on the dissolution of the fine particles, of which the body is composed. By the dissolution of these fine particles, illumination of the soul occurs and the member attains satisfaction and adopts the mind to perceive or realise the self. After the disappearance of rigor, identification with the soul takes place, the forces get dissolved into the theories and the self shines as self and enjoys happiness."

From that root came words such as *yozam* and yoga, and there are numerous compounds of that root in the Veda.The actual name of the Veda containing the yoga secrets is called the *'Yoga Veda'*. Swami Sivananda of Rishikesh refers to *shaman* yoga as 'London Yoga', which removes the diseases of the body and bestows upon the practitioner, practical good health. He opposes 'London Yoga' to 'Raja Yoga', the yoga that is set for spiritual attainment and development. The origin of Raja Yoga is found mostly in Patanjali Yoga Sutra of Patanjali and in later texts.

The term yoga is derived from the Sanskrit root 'Yuj', which means 'to unite' or 'to combine'. The origin of yoga is not known. However, it may be mentioned here that the word yoga is used both in the sense of a method of training or practice and in the sense of a state or realisation. For instance, it is used in the parable 'Chittavritti Nirodhah' of Patanjali commonly referred to in yoga lexicon.

Types of Yoga

Yoga encompasses a variety of practices aimed at achieving different objectives, ranging from physical health to spiritual growth. The major types include:

- *Hatha Yoga:* Focuses on physical postures and breath control.
- *Raja Yoga:* Known as the 'royal path', it focuses on meditation and strict adherence to the eight limbs of yoga.
- *Karma Yoga:* The path of selfless service.
- *Bhakti Yoga:* The path of devotion.
- *Jnana Yoga:* The path of wisdom and knowledge.
- *Mantra Yoga:* Involves chanting of mantras.
- *Laya Yoga:* Focuses on energy centres (chakras) and inner sound.

Definition of Applied Yoga

Applied yoga refers to the use of yoga principles and practices to achieve specific health-related goals, including disease prevention, management, and overall well-being. It integrates lifestyle modification tools of classical yoga into modern healthcare and daily life routines to promote physical, mental, and emotional health.

Scope of Applied Yoga in Modern Context

The scope of applied yoga in the modern context is vast. It includes its application in:

> Yoga, with its deep roots in ancient Indian traditions, has evolved into a versatile and holistic practice that addresses various aspects of modern life. Applied yoga, in particular, adapts classical yoga techniques to contemporary settings to promote physical, mental, and emotional well-being. This subdivision explores the diverse scope of applied yoga in the modern context, highlighting its integration into healthcare, education, corporate environments, sports, and community well-being.

Yoga in Healthcare

The integration of yoga into healthcare systems has gained significant momentum due to its comprehensive benefits. Applied yoga in healthcare focuses on using yoga techniques to complement traditional medical treatments, promote overall wellness, and prevent diseases. Many hospitals and healthcare facilities incorporate yoga as part of integrative medicine programs. These programs combine conventional medical treatments with complementary therapies like yoga to address various health conditions, including chronic pain, cardiovascular diseases, and mental health disorders.

Yoga is increasingly being used in rehabilitation settings to assist in recovery from surgeries, injuries, and illnesses. Specific yoga practices can help improve mobility, reduce pain, and enhance the overall quality of life for patients undergoing rehabilitation. Applied yoga is effective in managing mental health issues such as anxiety, depression, and PTSD. Yoga techniques like *pranayama* (breath control), meditation, and gentle *asanas* (postures) help reduce stress, improve mood, and promote emotional balance.

Yoga in Education

Incorporating yoga into educational settings offers numerous benefits for students, teachers, and administrators. Applied yoga in education enhances cognitive function, emotional regulation, and overall well-being. Yoga practices such as mindfulness and breathing exercises improve students' concentration and focus, leading to better academic performance and reduced classroom disruptions. The pressures of academic life can lead to stress and burnout. Applied yoga provides tools for stress management, helping students and teachers maintain emotional balance and resilience.

Regular yoga practice in schools promotes physical health by improving flexibility, strength, and posture. It also encourages a healthy lifestyle, reducing the risk of obesity and related health issues among students.

Yoga in Corporate Settings

The corporate world has embraced yoga as a means to enhance employee well-being, productivity, and workplace harmony. Applied yoga in corporate settings addresses the specific challenges of modern work environments. Yoga programmes in the workplace help reduce stress levels, improve mental clarity, and enhance overall job satisfaction. Techniques such as mindfulness meditation and stress-relief yoga sessions are particularly effective. By promoting physical and mental well-being, yoga can enhance employees' productivity and creativity. Regular practice improves concentration, reduces fatigue, and fosters a positive work environment. Corporate yoga sessions encourage teamwork and foster a sense of community among employees. These sessions can improve communication, trust, and collaboration within teams.

Yoga in Sports and Athletics

Athletes and sports enthusiasts increasingly recognize the benefits of yoga for enhancing performance, preventing injuries, and aiding recovery. Applied yoga in sports focuses on tailored practices to meet the specific needs of athletes. Yoga improves flexibility and strength, which are crucial for optimal athletic performance. Specific yoga poses target key muscle groups, enhancing overall physical capabilities. Mental focus and resilience are vital for athletes. Yoga practices like meditation and mindfulness improve mental clarity, concentration, and emotional resilience, helping athletes perform better under pressure. Yoga's emphasis on body awareness and balanced movement helps prevent injuries. Additionally, gentle yoga practices support recovery from intense training sessions and injuries, reducing downtime for athletes.

Yoga for Community Well-being

Applied yoga extends beyond individual benefits to promote community well-being. Community yoga programs foster social connections, inclusivity, and overall health in various populations. Yoga programmes tailored for seniors address the specific needs of older adults, promoting flexibility, balance, and joint health. These programmes also provide social interaction, reducing feelings of isolation. Yoga for children and teens supports physical development, emotional regulation, and social skills. Applied yoga in community centers and schools helps young people navigate the challenges of growing up. Yoga initiatives aimed at marginalised communities provide access to wellness practices that promote mental and physical health. These programmes can empower individuals, improve quality of life, and foster community resilience.

Yoga in Military and First Responder Settings

Applied yoga has found a valuable place in supporting the well-being of military personnel and first responders, who often face high-stress environments and traumatic experiences. Yoga techniques, including breath control and meditation, help military personnel and first responders manage stress and trauma. These practices can reduce symptoms of PTSD and enhance overall mental health. The physical demands of military and first responder duties require peak fitness levels. Yoga improves physical conditioning, flexibility, and strength, supporting the rigorous demands of these professions. Yoga fosters mental resilience and focus, essential qualities for military and first responder roles. Mindfulness practices enhance decision-making abilities and emotional regulation in high-pressure situations.

The scope of applied yoga in the modern context is vast and continually expanding. By integrating yoga into healthcare, education, corporate environments, sports, community programmes, and more, society can harness its holistic benefits to enhance overall well-being. Applied yoga's adaptability to various settings and populations underscores its relevance and potential to improve physical, mental, and emotional health in today's world. As yoga continues to evolve and adapt, its role in promoting a balanced, healthy, and harmonious life remains invaluable.

Objectives of Applied Yoga

Applied yoga offers numerous physical health benefits, including improved flexibility, strength, and endurance. It helps in the management of chronic conditions such as hypertension, diabetes, and arthritis.

Yoga, an ancient practice that originated in India thousands of years ago, has evolved into a global phenomenon celebrated for its extensive health benefits. Among its many advantages, yoga is particularly renowned for its positive impact on physical health. This portion delves into the myriad ways yoga contributes to physical well-being, emphasising how regular practice can enhance flexibility, strength, balance, and overall bodily function.

- *Improved Flexibility:* One of the most recognised benefits of yoga is its ability to enhance flexibility. Many yoga poses, such as Downward Dog (*Parvat-asana*) and Pigeon Pose (*Raj-Kapot-asana*), are specifically designed to stretch and lengthen muscles. Regular practice helps to increase the range of motion in joints and reduce stiffness. Improved flexibility can lead to better posture, reduce the risk of injury, and alleviate chronic pain, particularly in the back and shoulders. Yoga stretches muscles, tendons, and ligaments, promoting greater elasticity and reducing the likelihood of strains and sprains. Over time, as flexibility increases, movements become more fluid and less restricted. Chronic muscle tension, often caused by stress or prolonged periods of sitting, can lead to discomfort and pain. Yoga helps to release this tension through gentle stretching and relaxation techniques, contributing to a more comfortable and flexible body.
- *Increased Strength:* While yoga is often associated with flexibility, it also significantly enhances strength. Many yoga poses, such as Plank Pose and Warrior Poses (*Veer-bhadra-asana*), require holding the body in specific positions that help build muscle endurance and strength. Yoga heavily engages the core muscles, including the abdominals, obliques, and lower back. A strong core not only supports the spine but also enhances overall stability and balance. Different styles of yoga, particularly Ashtanga and Power Yoga, focus on dynamic sequences that help build strength across various muscle groups. This full-body strengthening helps in

maintaining muscle tone, supporting bone health, and improving metabolic function.

- *Better Balance:* Yoga enhances balance and coordination through various standing poses and sequences that challenge the body's stability. Improved balance is particularly beneficial for older adults, as it helps prevent falls and related injuries. Proprioception is the body's ability to sense its position and movement in space. Yoga enhances proprioception by requiring practitioners to maintain poses and transitions, thus improving overall body awareness and coordination. Enhanced balance and coordination from yoga translate to better functional mobility in daily activities. This includes improved walking gait, the ability to navigate uneven surfaces, and greater ease in performing everyday tasks.
- *Cardiovascular Health:* Yoga contributes to cardiovascular health by promoting relaxation and reducing stress, both of which are crucial for maintaining heart health. Additionally, dynamic forms of yoga can provide an aerobic workout, improving cardiovascular endurance. Certain yoga practices, such as deep breathing and meditation, can help lower blood pressure by inducing relaxation and reducing the stress hormone cortisol. Lower blood pressure reduces the risk of heart disease and stroke. Yoga enhances blood flow through a combination of physical movements and deep breathing leading to improved circulation. This improved ciculation helps in the efficient delivery of oxygen and nutrients to tissues and the removal of metabolic waste products.
- *Enhanced Respiratory Function:* Yoga places a strong emphasis on breath control, known as *pranayama*, which enhances respiratory efficiency and lung capacity. This can be particularly beneficial for individuals with respiratory conditions such as asthma or chronic bronchitis. *Pranayama* practices encourage deep diaphragmatic breathing, which increases oxygen intake and promotes relaxation. This type of breathing can help alleviate symptoms of anxiety and improve overall respiratory function. Regular practice of yoga can increase lung capacity and enhance the efficiency of the respiratory muscles. This leads to improved stamina and endurance, beneficial for both everyday activities and athletic performance.
- *Weight Management:* Yoga can play a supportive role in weight management by promoting physical activity, reducing stress, and encouraging mindfulness around eating habits. Dynamic forms of yoga, such as Vinyasa and Power Yoga, can provide a moderate to intense workout that burns calories and supports weight loss. Even

gentler forms of yoga can contribute to weight management by improving metabolic function. Yoga encourages mindfulness, which can extend to eating habits. Practitioners may become more aware of their body's hunger and satiety signals, leading to healthier food choices and better portion control.

- *Alleviation of Chronic Pain:* Yoga has been shown to alleviate various forms of chronic pain, including lower back pain, arthritis, and headaches. This is achieved through a combination of physical postures, breath control, and relaxation techniques.
  Yoga poses that stretch and strengthen the back muscles can alleviate chronic lower back pain. Poses such as Cat-Cow (*Marjari-asana*), Child's Pose (*Bal-asana*), and Sphinx Pose (*Salamb-Bhujang-asana*) are particularly effective for back pain relief.
  Gentle yoga can help manage arthritis by improving joint flexibility and reducing stiffness. Regular practice can decrease inflammation and increase mobility in affected joints.
- *Enhanced Athletic Performance*: Athletes can benefit from yoga through improved flexibility, strength, balance, and mental focus. Yoga can be an excellent complement to traditional athletic training, helping to prevent injuries and enhance overall performance. Yoga's emphasis on flexibility and balance helps reduce the risk of injuries in athletes. Stretching tight muscles and strengthening weak areas can create a more balanced and resilient body. Yoga also trains the mind to remain calm and focused, which is crucial for peak performance in sports. Techniques such as breath control and meditation can enhance concentration and mental clarity.

The physical health benefits of yoga are vast and well-documented. From improved flexibility and strength to better balance and cardiovascular health, yoga offers a holistic approach to physical well-being. Whether practiced as a standalone exercise or integrated into a broader fitness routine, yoga can enhance overall health and quality of life. By incorporating regular yoga practice into daily life, individuals can experience profound improvements in their physical health, paving the way for a more active, balanced, and fulfilling life.

Mental Health Benefits of Practicing Yoga

Yoga practices such as meditation and breath control help in reducing stress, anxiety, and depression. They enhance cognitive function and mental clarity, contributing to overall mental well-being.

Yoga is a multifaceted practice that benefits not only physical health but also plays a significant role in enhancing mental well-being. The practice of yoga has been associated with numerous positive outcomes on mental health, including stress reduction and mood improvement. By engaging in yoga, individuals can experience a shift in their body's response from the sympathetic nervous system to the parasympathetic system, promoting a relaxation response that has calming and restorative effects. This shift towards the parasympathetic system can lead to lower heart rates, decreased blood pressure, reduced cortisol levels, and increased blood flow to vital organs and intestines, all of which contribute to an overall sense of psychological well-being. Additionally, yoga has been found to be effective in helping individuals manage stress, develop coping skills, and cultivate a more positive outlook on life. Furthermore, regular practice of yoga has been linked to improved sleep quality, decreased time taken to fall asleep, and increased total hours of sleep, demonstrating its potential to positively impact mental health through improved sleep patterns. Overall, the holistic nature of yoga makes it a valuable tool for nurturing both the mind and body, offering individuals a respite from the demands of daily life and supporting their journey towards improved mental well-being.

Applied yoga fosters emotional balance by promoting relaxation and emotional resilience. It helps individuals manage emotions more effectively, leading to improved relationships and a more positive outlook on life.

Yoga, an ancient practice with roots in Indian philosophy, has become a global phenomenon recognised for its profound impact on both physical and emotional health. While the physical benefits of yoga are widely acknowledged, its contributions to emotional well-being are equally significant. This portion explores how yoga fosters emotional well-being, examining the mechanisms through which it reduces stress, enhances mood, promotes emotional resilience, and cultivates mindfulness.

Reduction of Stress and Anxiety

One of the most notable benefits of yoga is its ability to reduce stress and anxiety. Modern life is often characterised by high levels of stress, which can lead to various emotional and physical health issues. Yoga provides an effective tool for managing and alleviating stress through its combination of physical postures, breath control, and meditation.

Yoga activates the parasympathetic nervous system, also known as the "rest and digest" system. Practices such as deep breathing, gentle stretches, and relaxation postures calm the nervous system, reducing the production of stress hormones like cortisol. This leads to a state of relaxation and decreased anxiety levels. *Pranayama*, or breath control, is a core component of yoga that significantly contributes to stress reduction. Techniques such as diaphragmatic breathing, alternate nostril breathing, and *Ujjayi* breathing help calm the mind, reduce heart rate, and lower blood pressure. These practices promote a sense of calm and relaxation, making it easier to cope with stress and anxiety.

Enhancement of Mood

Yoga has been shown to enhance mood and combat symptoms of depression. The combination of physical activity, mindfulness, and controlled breathing helps release endorphins, the body's natural mood elevators.

Physical activity in yoga stimulates the release of endorphins, which are neurotransmitters that promote feelings of happiness and well-being. The gentle, rhythmic movements and mindful focus of yoga enhance this effect, leading to improved mood and emotional balance. Yoga influences the balance of neurotransmitters in the brain, including serotonin and gamma-aminobutyric acid (GABA). Increased levels of these neurotransmitters are associated with reduced anxiety and depression, contributing to overall emotional well-being.

Promotion of Emotional Resilience

Emotional resilience refers to the ability to adapt to stressful situations and bounce back from adversity. Yoga builds emotional resilience through its emphasis on mindfulness, self-awareness, and acceptance. Mindfulness is a fundamental aspect of yoga, encouraging practitioners to focus on the present moment without judgment. This practice helps individuals become more aware of their thoughts and emotions, allowing them to respond to stressors with greater clarity and composure. Yoga teaches the principles of acceptance and non-attachment, which are essential for emotional resilience. By accepting situations as they are and letting go of the need to control outcomes, individuals can navigate life's challenges with a more balanced and resilient mindset.

Cultivation of Mindfulness

Mindfulness, the practice of being fully present in the moment, is central to yoga. This practice has been shown to enhance emotional well-being by reducing rumination, improving focus, and fostering a greater sense of peace.

Rumination, or the repetitive focus on negative thoughts, is a common contributor to emotional distress. Mindfulness practices in yoga help break this cycle by redirecting attention to the present moment and promoting a non-judgmental awareness of thoughts and feelings. Regular mindfulness practice improves focus and concentration, which can enhance overall emotional well-being. A clear and focused mind is better equipped to handle stress, make decisions, and maintain emotional balance.

Emotional Expression and Release

Yoga provides a safe and supportive environment for emotional expression and release. Certain poses and practices are specifically designed to unlock and release stored emotions, promoting emotional healing and balance. Poses such as Camel Pose, Cobra Pose, and Bridge Pose are known as heart-opening poses. These postures open the chest and release tension in the upper body, which can help to release stored emotions and promote emotional openness and vulnerability. Trauma-informed yoga is a specialised approach that recognises the impact of trauma on the body and mind. It incorporates gentle, supportive practices that help individuals safely explore and release trauma-related emotions, promoting emotional healing and resilience.

Connection and Community

Yoga fosters a sense of connection and community, which is essential for emotional well-being. Group classes and yoga communities provide a supportive environment where individuals can connect with others, share experiences, and build meaningful relationships.

Participation in yoga classes and communities provides social support, which is a key factor in emotional well-being. The sense of belonging and connection with others can reduce feelings of loneliness and isolation, enhancing overall emotional health. Sharing the practice of yoga with others creates a sense of camaraderie and mutual support. The shared experience of practicing yoga can build strong bonds and foster a sense of unity and collective well-being.

Self-Compassion and Self-Awareness

Yoga promotes self-compassion and self-awareness, encouraging individuals to treat themselves with kindness and understanding. This shift in mindset can lead to improved emotional well-being and a more positive self-image. Yoga encourages practitioners to listen to their bodies, respect their limits, and approach themselves with compassion. This practice fosters a kinder and more forgiving attitude towards oneself, reducing self-criticism and enhancing emotional well-being.

Through mindful movement and introspection, yoga enhances self-awareness. This increased awareness allows individuals to recognise and understand their emotions, leading to greater emotional intelligence and the ability to manage emotions more effectively.

Yoga's impact on emotional well-being is profound and multifaceted. Through the reduction of stress and anxiety, enhancement of mood, promotion of emotional resilience, and cultivation of mindfulness, yoga provides a holistic approach to emotional health. Additionally, yoga encourages emotional expression and release, fosters connection and community, and promotes self-compassion and self-awareness. By integrating yoga into daily life, individuals can experience significant improvements in their emotional well-being, leading to a more balanced, peaceful, and fulfilling life.

Spiritual Growth Induced by Yoga Practices

While the primary focus of applied yoga in the modern context is often on physical and mental health, it also supports spiritual growth by encouraging self-awareness, mindfulness, and a deeper connection with one's inner self.

Yoga, a practice that transcends mere physical exercise, offers profound pathways to spiritual growth. Rooted in ancient Indian philosophy, yoga encompasses practices that aim to unite the body, mind, and spirit. This holistic approach facilitates a deep inner transformation, fostering a greater sense of self-awareness, inner peace, and connection to a higher consciousness. This part explores how yoga induces spiritual growth through its various practices and philosophical teachings.

At its core, yoga is a spiritual discipline that aims to achieve union with the divine or a higher state of consciousness. The word 'yoga' is derived from the Sanskrit root 'Yuj', meaning 'to yoke' or 'to unite'. This union refers to the merging of the individual self with the universal consciousness. Yoga's spiritual dimension is integral to its practice, and it manifests through various forms, including meditation, ethical living, and self-inquiry.

The spiritual aspects of yoga are well articulated in the Yoga Sutras of Patanjali, which outline the Eight Limbs of Yoga:

1. *Yamas (Ethical Disciplines):* Guidelines for moral and ethical conduct.
2. *Niyamas (Personal Observances):* Practices for self-discipline and spiritual observance.
3. *Asanas (Postures):* Physical postures to prepare the body for meditation.
4. *Pranayama (Breath Control):* Techniques to control the breath and life force.
5. *Pratyahara (Withdrawal of Senses):* Turning inward and detaching from sensory distractions.
6. *Dharana (Concentration):* Focused concentration on a single point or object.
7. *Dhyana (Meditation):* Sustained meditation leading to deeper awareness.
8. *Samadhi (Union/ Libereation):* The ultimate state of spiritual absorption and enlightenment.

Each limb contributes to the practitioner's spiritual journey, fostering growth and transformation.

Yoga practices, particularly meditation and mindfulness, cultivate deep self-awareness. This heightened awareness allows individuals to observe their thoughts, emotions, and behaviours without judgment, leading to greater self-understanding and spiritual insight.

Meditation is a cornerstone of yoga that promotes inner reflection and mindfulness. Regular meditation practice helps to quiet the mind, reduce mental chatter, and create space for introspection. This process of turning inward facilitates a deeper understanding of one's true nature and the underlying unity of all existence. Mindfulness, an integral part of yoga, encourages practitioners to live in the present moment with full awareness. This practice extends beyond the yoga mat, influencing daily activities and interactions. By being mindful, individuals develop a deeper connection to their inner self and the world around them, fostering spiritual growth.

Connection to the Divine

Yoga serves as a bridge between the individual and the divine. Through various practices, individuals experience a sense of connection to a higher power or universal consciousness, leading to spiritual awakening and growth.

Bhakti Yoga: Path of Devotion

Bhakti Yoga emphasises devotion and love for the divine. This path involves practices such as chanting, prayer, and rituals, which help to cultivate a deep sense of devotion and surrender. Through these practices, individuals experience a profound connection to the divine, fostering spiritual growth.

Mantra Yoga: Power of Sacred Sounds

Mantra Yoga involves the repetition of sacred sounds or phrases (mantras). These mantras are believed to have vibrational frequencies that align the individual with higher states of consciousness. Regular chanting or silent repetition of mantras deepens the spiritual experience, promoting inner peace and connection to the divine.

Ethical and Moral Living

The ethical and moral guidelines outlined in the Yamas and Niyamas form the foundation of yoga practice. Adhering to these principles fosters spiritual growth by promoting virtuous living and aligning one's actions with higher ethical standards.

The Yamas are ethical guidelines that include non-violence (*ahimsa*), truthfulness (*satya*), non-stealing (*asteya*), sexual restraint (*brahmacharya*), and non-possessiveness (*aparigraha*). Practicing these disciplines cultivates moral integrity and spiritual purity.

The Niyamas are personal observances that include cleanliness (*shaucha*), contentment (*santosha*), self-discipline (*tapas*), self-study (*svadhyaya*), and surrender to a higher power (*ishvara pranidhana*). These practices foster inner discipline and spiritual devotion, facilitating spiritual growth.

Yoga practices such as *asanas*, *pranayama*, and *kriyas* (cleansing techniques) purify the body and mind, transforming energy and facilitating spiritual growth. *Asanas*, or physical postures, are designed to prepare the body for meditation by promoting physical health and flexibility. They also help to release stored tension and energy blockages, allowing the life force (*prana*) to flow freely. *Pranayama* involves breath control techniques that enhance the flow of prana and purify the energy channels (*nadis*). By regulating the breath, practitioners balance their energy and promote mental clarity, paving the way for spiritual experiences. Kriyas are cleansing practices that purify the body and mind, removing toxins and negative energies. These techniques include nasal cleansing (*neti*), digestive cleansing (*dhauti*), and other practices that support physical and energetic purification.

Unity and Oneness

The ultimate goal of yoga is to experience the unity and oneness of all existence. This realisation of interconnectedness fosters a sense of compassion, love, and harmony with the world, contributing to profound spiritual growth.

Samadhi, the final limb of Patanjali's Eight Limbs of Yoga, represents the state of spiritual absorption and enlightenment. In this state, the individual self merges with the universal consciousness, experiencing the ultimate unity and oneness. As individuals progress on their spiritual path, they develop a greater sense of compassion and a desire to serve others. This selfless service, known as Karma Yoga, enhances spiritual growth by fostering a sense of unity and interconnectedness with all beings.

Yoga's potential to induce spiritual growth is immense and multifaceted. Through practices that cultivate self-awareness, connect to the divine, promote ethical living, purify the body and mind, and foster a sense of unity, yoga provides a holistic pathway to spiritual transformation. By integrating these practices into daily life, individuals can experience profound spiritual growth, leading to a more enlightened, peaceful, and fulfilling existence.

Practical Applications of Applied Yoga

Applied yoga, an adaptation of traditional yoga practices to modern contexts, serves as a powerful tool to enhance physical, mental, and emotional well-being. Its practical applications span various sectors, including healthcare, education, corporate environments, sports, community services, and digital platforms. This comprehensive section explores the diverse practical applications of applied yoga, highlighting its benefits and innovative uses in contemporary settings.

Yoga in Healthcare

Applied yoga has become an integral component of modern healthcare, offering complementary therapies for various physical and mental health conditions. Its practical applications in healthcare are extensive and multifaceted. Healthcare facilities integrate yoga into their treatment plans to complement conventional medical treatments, addressing chronic pain, cardiovascular health, cancer support, and more.

- *Chronic Pain Management:* Yoga helps alleviate chronic pain conditions such as arthritis, fibromyalgia, and lower back pain through gentle stretching, strengthening exercises, and relaxation techniques.
- *Cardiovascular Health:* Yoga practices help lower blood pressure and improve heart health by promoting relaxation and reducing stress. Yoga is increasingly being used to treat mental health conditions like anxiety, depression, and PTSD. Techniques such as meditation, breath control, and restorative yoga support emotional regulation and mental clarity. Mindfulness-Based Stress Reduction (MBSR): Combining yoga and mindfulness meditation to reduce stress and improve mental health.
- *Trauma-Informed Yoga:* Specialised yoga practices designed for individuals with trauma histories, providing a safe space for healing. Yoga aids in rehabilitation programmes, enhancing physical recovery from surgeries, injuries, and illnesses while supporting mental recovery through relaxation and stress management techniques.
- *Post-Surgery Recovery:* Gentle yoga practices improve mobility and reduce post-operative pain.
- *Injury Rehabilitation:* Yoga supports the healing process by enhancing flexibility, strength, and balance.

Yoga in Education

In educational settings, yoga enhances cognitive function, emotional regulation, and overall well-being for students, teachers, and administrators. Schools incorporate yoga into the curriculum to improve focus, behaviour, and academic performance.

- *Mindfulness Exercises:* Short, daily mindfulness practices help students concentrate and reduce anxiety.
- *Physical Education Classes:* Yoga is included in physical education to promote physical health and teach relaxation techniques. Training teachers in yoga techniques equips them with tools to manage classroom stress and enhance their own well-being.
- *Stress Management:* Techniques for teachers to reduce stress and prevent burnout.
- *Classroom Management:* Yoga-based strategies to create a calm and focused learning environment. Yoga is adapted for children with special needs to support their physical and emotional development.

- *Sensory Integration:* Activities that enhance sensory processing and motor skills.
- *Emotional Regulation:* Techniques to help children manage their emotions and behaviour.

Yoga in Corporate Settings

The corporate world has embraced yoga to enhance employee well-being, productivity, and workplace harmony. Applied yoga addresses the specific challenges of modern work environments. Many companies offer yoga as part of their employee wellness programs.

- *On-Site Yoga Classes:* Regular yoga sessions at the workplace to reduce stress and improve physical health.
- *Virtual Yoga Sessions:* Online classes for remote employees to maintain wellness practices from home.
- Yoga practices such as mindfulness meditation and relaxation techniques help reduce workplace stress and improve mental clarity. Yoga sessions are used as team-building activities to improve communication, trust, and collaboration among employees.
- *Retreats and Workshops:* Corporate retreats that include yoga can foster a sense of community and collective well-being.

Yoga in Sports and Athletics

Athletes and sports enthusiasts utilise yoga to enhance performance, prevent injuries, and aid recovery. Yoga is incorporated into training programmes to improve athletes' flexibility and strength.

- *Dynamic Stretching:* Enhancing muscle elasticity and joint mobility.
- *Core Strength:* Building core stability and strength to support athletic performance. Yoga enhances mental focus and resilience, essential qualities for athletes.
- *Meditation:* Techniques to improve concentration and reduce stress during competitions. Yoga helps prevent injuries by promoting balanced muscle development and improving body awareness.
- *Recovery Practices:* Gentle yoga supports recovery from intense training sessions and injuries, reducing downtime.

Yoga for Community Well-being

Applied yoga promotes community well-being by fostering social connections, inclusivity, and overall health in various populations. Community centres and retirement homes offer yoga programs tailored for seniors.

- *Gentle Yoga:* Low-impact exercises to improve mobility and balance.
- *Chair Yoga:* Accessible yoga practices performed seated, suitable for those with limited mobility. Yoga programmes in community centres and schools support physical, emotional, and social development in young people.
- *Story-Based Yoga:* Integrating yoga poses with storytelling to engage young children.
- *Yoga for Stress Relief:* Techniques to help teens manage academic and social pressures. Yoga initiatives aimed at marginalised communities provide access to wellness practices that promote mental and physical health.
- *Trauma-Informed Yoga:* Supporting individuals who have experienced trauma.
- *Accessible Yoga:* Adapting practices for individuals with disabilities.

Yoga in Digital and Virtual Platforms

The digital age has expanded the reach of yoga, making it accessible to a global audience through online platforms. Digital or virtual platforms offer a variety of yoga classes accessible to people worldwide.

- *Beginner to Advanced Levels:* Classes cater to different skill levels and styles.
- *Specialized Programs:* Focused on specific needs such as stress relief, flexibility, and strength.
- Yoga apps provide guided practices, meditation sessions, and wellness tips. Some innovative apps use virtual reality to create immersive yoga experiences.
- *Personalised Programmes:* Apps offer personalized yoga routines based on individual goals and preferences.
- *Interactive Features:* Virtual reality can enhance the practice by providing interactive and engaging environments. Yoga is integrated into telehealth and online therapy sessions, providing remote support for mental health and well-being.
- *Virtual Consultations:* Practitioners guide clients through yoga practices tailored to their therapeutic needs.
- *Remote Wellness Programs:* Online programmes offer continuous support for mental and physical health.

The practical applications of applied yoga in modern contexts are extensive and continually expanding. By integrating yoga into healthcare, education, corporate environments, sports, community programs, and digital platforms, society can harness its holistic benefits to enhance overall well-being. The adaptability of applied yoga to various settings and populations underscores its relevance and potential to improve physical, mental, and emotional health in today's world. As yoga continues to evolve and adapt, its role in promoting a balanced, healthy, and harmonious life remains invaluable.

Challenges and Limitations of Applied Yoga

While applied yoga offers numerous benefits and practical applications across various sectors, it also faces several challenges and limitations. These challenges can affect the effectiveness and acceptance of yoga practices in modern contexts. This artefact explores the key challenges and limitations of applied yoga, highlighting issues such as cultural appropriation, lack of standardisation, accessibility, scientific validation, and the commercial aspects of yoga.

Cultural Appropriation, Misrepresentation and Dilution

- One of the major challenges of applied yoga is cultural appropriation. Yoga, with its deep roots in Indian spiritual and philosophical traditions, is often misrepresented or diluted when adapted to different cultural contexts.
- *Commercialisation*: The commercialisation of yoga in the West sometimes leads to the loss of its spiritual essence, reducing it to mere physical exercise.
- *Superficial Practices:* Some modern interpretations of yoga focus solely on the physical aspects, neglecting the holistic and spiritual dimensions that are integral to traditional yoga. The appropriation of yoga without acknowledging its cultural and historical origins can be seen as disrespectful.
- *Acknowledgment of Source:* There is a need for greater awareness and respect for the cultural heritage of yoga, ensuring that its practices honour the traditions from which they originate.

Lack of Standardisation

The absence of standardised training and certification processes for yoga instructors can lead to inconsistencies in the quality of instruction.

- *Varied Standards:* Different organisations and schools have varying standards for certifying yoga teachers, resulting in a wide range of expertise and competence.

- *Quality Control:* Without standardised guidelines, the quality of yoga instruction can vary significantly, affecting the safety and effectiveness of the practice.
- The diversity of yoga styles and schools adds to the complexity of standardising applied yoga practices.
- *Confusion for Practitioners:* The plethora of yoga styles can confuse practitioners, making it challenging to choose the appropriate style that meets their needs and goals.

Socio-economic Barriers or Accessibility Issues

Access to yoga can be limited by socioeconomic factors, making it difficult for certain populations to benefit from its practices.

- *Cost of Classes:* High costs associated with yoga classes, workshops, and retreats can be prohibitive for low-income individuals.
- *Limited Availability:* In some areas, especially rural or underserved communities, there may be limited access to qualified yoga instructors and facilities. Not all yoga practices are accessible to individuals with physical limitations or disabilities.
- *Adaptation Challenges:* Adapting yoga practices to accommodate different physical abilities requires specialized training and knowledge, which may not always be available.
- *Inclusivity:* Ensuring that yoga is inclusive and accessible to people of all ages, sizes, and physical conditions remains a significant challenge.

Limited Research or Scientific Validation

While there is a growing body of research supporting the benefits of yoga, more scientific studies are needed to fully validate its efficacy for various health conditions.

- *Lack of Rigorous Studies:* Many existing studies on yoga are limited by small sample sizes, lack of control groups, and other methodological issues.
- *Need for Evidence-Based Practices:* Greater emphasis on rigorous, evidence-based research is necessary to substantiate the therapeutic claims of applied yoga. Integrating yoga with conventional medical treatments requires a solid foundation of scientific evidence.
- *Medical Acceptance:* For yoga to be widely accepted in medical communities, more robust research and clinical trials are needed to demonstrate its effectiveness and safety.

Commercialisation of Yoga

The commercialisation of yoga has led to a focus on profit rather than the holistic and therapeutic aspects of the practice.

- *Yoga as a Trend:* The trendiness of yoga can lead to the creation of yoga products and services that prioritise profit over genuine well-being.
- *Dilution of Authenticity:* The essence of yoga can be lost when commercial interests overshadow its traditional values and principles. The rapid growth of the yoga industry has resulted in market saturation, with numerous studios and instructors competing for clientele.
- *Quality Over Quantity:* In the rush to capitalise on the popularity of yoga, the quality of instruction and the depth of practice can suffer.
- *Consumer Confusion:* With so many options available, consumers may struggle to identify authentic and high-quality yoga practices.

Despite its numerous benefits and widespread applications, applied yoga faces several challenges and limitations that can impact its effectiveness and acceptance in modern contexts. Addressing issues such as cultural appropriation, lack of standardisation, accessibility, scientific validation, and commercialisation is crucial for ensuring that yoga remains a holistic, inclusive, and effective practice. By acknowledging and overcoming these challenges, the full potential of applied yoga can be realised, promoting well-being and health across diverse populations and settings.

Summary

Applied yoga, rooted in ancient wisdom, offers significant benefits for physical, mental, and emotional health. It integrates classical yoga principles into modern contexts, enhancing overall well-being and supporting disease management. Despite challenges such as cultural appropriation and lack of standardisation, applied yoga continues to be a valuable tool in promoting health and well-being in various settings, including healthcare, education, and corporate environments. By sincerely applying yogic principles, individuals can reap the extensive benefits of this ancient practice.

2

Application of Bhakti, Gyan, Karma, Raja and Hatha Yoga

Yoga, an ancient practice rooted in Indian philosophy and spirituality, offers a comprehensive system for personal development and self-realisation. Over millennia, different paths of yoga have evolved, each emphasising unique aspects of spiritual practice and personal growth. These paths—Bhakti Yoga, Gyan Yoga, Karma Yoga, Raja Yoga, and Hatha Yoga—provide diverse methodologies to suit various temperaments, lifestyles, and goals. Understanding and applying these distinct forms of yoga can profoundly impact one's physical, mental, and spiritual well-being.

Bhakti Yoga: The Path of Devotion

Bhakti Yoga, often referred to as the yoga of devotion, centers on cultivating of a deep, personal relationship with the divine. This path emphasises love, devotion, and surrender to a higher power, typically personified in a chosen deity. Practitioners of Bhakti Yoga engage in devotional practices such as chanting, singing hymns, prayer, and rituals, which foster a sense of connection and unity with the divine.

Practical Application

- *Daily Devotional Practices:* Incorporating activities like chanting mantras, participating in kirtans (devotional singing), and performing pujas (ritual worship) into daily life.
- *Cultivating Compassion and Humility:* Emphasising selfless love and service to others as a form of worship, thereby promoting compassion and humility.
- *Fostering Community:* Participating in religious gatherings and community services to enhance the sense of belonging and shared spiritual pursuit.

Gyan Yoga: Path of Knowledge

Gyan (Jnana) Yoga, the path of knowledge and wisdom, focuses on intellectual and philosophical inquiry into the nature of reality and the self. It involves deep contemplation, self-study, and meditation to discern the true nature of existence and attain spiritual enlightenment. This path is suited for those with a keen interest in philosophy and a contemplative disposition.

Practical Application

- *Scriptural Study:* Engaging in the study of sacred texts such as the *Upanishads*, *Bhagavad Gita*, and *Vedanta* philosophy to gain insight into spiritual truths.
- *Self-Inquiry (Atma Vichara):* Practicing self-reflection and questioning the nature of the self and reality through techniques like "Who am I?" meditation.
- *Guided Discussions:* Participating in *satsangs* (spiritual gatherings) and discussions with knowledgeable teachers to deepen understanding and clarify doubts.

Karma Yoga: Path of Selfless Action

Karma Yoga, the path of selfless action, emphasises performing one's duties and actions without attachment to the results. It teaches the principles of altruism and service, encouraging practitioners to dedicate their efforts to the greater good and the welfare of others. This path integrates spirituality into daily life through ethical living and selfless service.

Practical Application

- *Service to Others:* Volunteering in community service, helping those in need, and engaging in charitable activities without expecting anything in return.
- *Mindful Work:* Performing daily tasks with full attention and dedication, viewing work as a form of worship.
- *Ethical Living:* Upholding ethical principles and integrity in all actions, fostering a sense of responsibility and purpose.

Raja Yoga: Path of Meditation

Raja Yoga, known as the royal path, emphasises meditation and mental discipline as the means to attain spiritual enlightenment. It is systematically outlined in Patanjali's Yoga Sutras, which describe an eightfold path (*Ashtanga Yoga*) that includes ethical guidelines, physical postures, breath control, and various stages of meditation leading to self-realisation.

Practical Application

- *Ashtanga Practice:* Following the eightfold path, which includes *Yama* (ethical disciplines), *Niyama* (personal observances), *Asana* (postures), *Pranayama* (breath control), *Pratyahara* (withdrawal of senses), *Dharana* (concentration), *Dhyana* (meditation), and *Samadhi* (absorption).
- *Daily Meditation:* Establishing a consistent meditation practice to cultivate inner peace and mental clarity.
- *Mindfulness and Concentration:* Developing mindfulness in daily activities and practicing concentration techniques to enhance focus and awareness.

Hatha Yoga: Path of Physical Discipline

Hatha Yoga, often associated with physical postures and exercises, aims to prepare the body and mind for higher spiritual practices. It combines *asanas* (physical postures), *pranayama* (breathing techniques), and cleansing practices to purify the body, balance energy, and cultivate physical and mental strength.

Practical Application

- *Asana Practice:* Regularly practicing physical postures to improve flexibility, strength, and overall health.
- *Pranayama:* Incorporating breathing exercises to enhance respiratory function, balance energy, and calm the mind.
- *Shatkarma* (Cleansing Techniques)*:* Practicing traditional cleansing techniques to detoxify and purify the body, promoting overall well-being.

The diverse paths of Bhakti, Gyan, Karma, Raja, and Hatha Yoga offer comprehensive frameworks for spiritual growth and personal development. Each path caters to different temperaments and inclinations, allowing individuals to choose the practices that resonate most deeply with them. By integrating these yoga practices into daily life, individuals can achieve a harmonious balance of body, mind, and spirit, leading to profound transformations and a deeper connection with the self and the universe.

Bhakti Yoga in Modern Era

Bhakti Yoga, the path of devotion, has been practiced for centuries as a means to cultivate a deep, personal connection with the divine. Rooted in ancient Indian spiritual traditions, Bhakti Yoga focuses on love, devotion, and surrender to a higher power. Despite its ancient origins, Bhakti Yoga remains highly relevant in the modern era, offering profound benefits for individuals and communities alike. This artefact explores the application and relevance of Bhakti Yoga in today's world, highlighting how its principles and practices can enhance personal well-being and foster a sense of connectedness in an increasingly fragmented society.

Understanding Bhakti Yoga

Bhakti Yoga is one of the major paths to spiritual realisation, alongside Karma Yoga (the path of selfless action), Gyan Yoga (the path of knowledge), and Raja Yoga (the path of meditation). The term "*Bhakti*" comes from the Sanskrit word for "devotion" or "love," and Bhakti Yoga involves practices that express love and devotion towards the divine. This path is accessible to all, regardless of one's background or religious affiliation, as it emphasises an emotional connection with the divine rather than intellectual or physical prowess.

Core Principles of Bhakti Yoga

- *Love and Devotion:* Central to Bhakti Yoga is the unconditional love and devotion towards a chosen deity or the divine in a personal form.
- *Surrender:* Surrendering one's ego and desires to the divine, acknowledging that there is a higher power guiding and supporting us.
- *Selflessness:* Cultivating selfless love and compassion for others as an expression of one's devotion.

Common Practices in Bhakti Yoga

- *Kirtan and Bhajan*: Singing devotional songs and hymns.
- *Japa*: Repetition of divine names or mantras.
- *Puja and Rituals*: Performing daily worship and offering rituals.

- *Satsang*: Gathering with other devotees to share spiritual experiences and insights.
- *Scriptural Study*: Reading and reflecting on sacred texts that emphasise devotion, such as the *Bhagavad Gita*, *Ramayana*, and *Srimad Bhagavatam*.

Application of Bhakti Yoga in the Modern Era

Bhakti Yoga offers numerous applications for enhancing personal and communal well-being in the contemporary world. Its practices can be seamlessly integrated into daily life, providing emotional, psychological, and social benefits. In today's fast-paced and stressful world, Bhakti Yoga offers a sanctuary for emotional healing and mental peace. The practices of Bhakti Yoga, such as chanting and singing, have been shown to have a calming effect on the mind, reducing stress and anxiety.

- *Stress Reduction:* Regular participation in devotional singing and chanting can lower cortisol levels, the body's primary stress hormone, leading to reduced stress and anxiety.
- *Emotional Resilience:* The practice of surrender and acceptance in Bhakti Yoga helps individuals develop emotional resilience, enabling them to cope better with life's challenges.
- *Inner Peace:* Devotional practices foster a sense of inner peace and contentment, providing a refuge from the pressures of modern life.

Bhakti Yoga fosters a sense of community and belonging, which is crucial in an era where social isolation and loneliness are prevalent. The communal aspects of Bhakti Yoga, such as group chanting (*kirtan*) and shared rituals, help build strong social bonds.

- *Community Building*: Participating in group devotional activities creates a sense of community and support, reducing feelings of loneliness and isolation.
- *Cultural Preservation*: Bhakti Yoga helps preserve and promote cultural traditions and values, fostering a sense of identity and continuity.
- *Service and Compassion:* The emphasis on selfless love and compassion in Bhakti Yoga encourages community service and social responsibility.

Bhakti Yoga provides a clear and accessible path for personal spiritual growth, regardless of one's religious background. It emphasises direct experience and personal connection with the divine, making it relevant for people from diverse spiritual traditions.

- *Universal Appeal:* Bhakti Yoga's focus on love and devotion transcends religious boundaries, making it accessible and relevant to people of all faiths.
- *Holistic Development:* The integration of emotional, mental, and spiritual practices in Bhakti Yoga promotes holistic personal development.
- *Guided Spiritual Practice:* Bhakti Yoga offers structured practices and rituals that provide a clear framework for spiritual growth and development.

Relevance of Bhakti Yoga in Modern Times

The relevance of Bhakti Yoga in the modern era lies in its ability to address some of the key challenges faced by individuals and society today. Its timeless principles and practices offer solutions to contemporary issues, making it a valuable and transformative practice.

In an age where materialism and consumerism often overshadow deeper values, many people experience a sense of meaninglessness and lack of purpose. Bhakti Yoga addresses this crisis by providing a profound sense of purpose through devotion and service to the divine.

- *Sense of Purpose:* Devotion to a higher power gives individuals a sense of purpose and direction in life.
- *Fulfilment and Satisfaction:* The selfless love and service inherent in Bhakti Yoga lead to deeper fulfilment and satisfaction than material pursuits.

Bhakti Yoga cultivates emotional intelligence by encouraging the expression and management of emotions through devotional practices. This emotional maturity is essential for personal well-being and effective social interactions.

- *Empathy and Compassion:* The practice of Bhakti Yoga enhances empathy and compassion, key components of emotional intelligence.
- *Emotional Regulation:* Devotional practices help individuals manage and regulate their emotions, leading to greater emotional stability.

Mental health issues, such as anxiety, depression, and stress, are prevalent in modern society. Bhakti Yoga offers practical tools to promote mental health and well-being.

- *Mindfulness and Presence:* The focus on mindfulness and presence in devotional practices helps reduce anxiety and depression.
- *Positive Emotional States:* Bhakti Yoga promotes positive emotional states such as love, joy, and gratitude, which are essential for mental health.

The principles of love, compassion, and selflessness in Bhakti Yoga have the potential to foster global harmony and peace. By encouraging individuals to see the divine in all beings, Bhakti Yoga promotes a sense of unity and interconnectedness.

- *Universal Brotherhood*: Bhakti Yoga's emphasis on seeing the divine in everyone fosters a sense of universal brotherhood and sisterhood.
- *Peaceful Coexistence*: The principles of non-violence and compassion in Bhakti Yoga contribute to peaceful coexistence and conflict resolution.

Bhakti Yoga, with its emphasis on love, devotion, and selfless service, remains highly relevant and applicable in the modern era. Its practices offer profound benefits for emotional and mental well-being, social and community connection, and personal spiritual growth. By addressing contemporary challenges such as the crisis of meaning, mental health issues, and social isolation, Bhakti Yoga provides timeless solutions that can transform individuals and society. Embracing the principles and practices of Bhakti Yoga can lead to a more compassionate, peaceful, and fulfilled life, underscoring its enduring relevance in today's world.

Qualities of a Bhakta (Devotee)

a. According to the Narada Bhakti Sutra

The qualities of a devotee (*bhakta*) as described in the Narada Bhakti Sutra and the *Bhagavad Gita* provide profound insights into the nature of true devotion. Both texts highlight the essential characteristics that a *bhakta* should embody to achieve a higher spiritual state. Below is an exploration of these qualities as outlined in these two revered scriptures.

- The Narada Bhakti Sutra is a classical text that outlines the philosophy and practice of Bhakti Yoga. It emphasises pure, selfless devotion to the divine. The qualities of a *bhakta* as described in this text include:
- *Pure Love (Ananya Bhakti):* The primary quality of a *bhakta* is unwavering, exclusive devotion to the divine. This love is free from any selfish desires or expectations of reward.
- *Humility (Dainya):* A true devotee remains humble, recognising their dependence on the divine. They do not seek personal glory or recognition.
- *Compassion (Karuna):* A *bhakta* shows compassion and empathy towards all living beings. They are moved by the suffering of others and strive to alleviate it.
- *Non-attachment (Virakti):* Devotees practice non-attachment to material possessions and outcomes, focusing solely on their love and service to the divine.
- *Steadfastness (Nishchala Bhakti):* The devotion of a *bhakta* remains steadfast and unwavering, regardless of external circumstances or challenges.
- *Inner Joy (Ananda):* A *bhakta* experiences inner joy and bliss from their connection with the divine, independent of external pleasures or pains.
- *Faith (Shraddha):* Strong, unwavering faith in the divine and the path of devotion is a key quality of a *bhakta*. This faith sustains them through all trials and tribulations.
- *Purity (Shuddhi):* Purity of heart, mind, and actions is essential. A *bhakta* strives to lead a life of moral integrity and virtue.

b. According to the Bhagavad Gita

The *Bhagavad Gita*, a dialogue between Lord Krishna and Arjuna, outlines the qualities of a true devotee in various chapters, especially in Chapter 12 (Bhakti Yoga). Some of the key qualities mentioned include:

- *Equanimity (Samattvam):* A *bhakta* remains balanced and composed in both joy and sorrow, success and failure. They are not disturbed by the dualities of life (Chapter 12, Verse 13).

- *Freedom from Malice (Adveshta):* A true devotee harbors no ill-will or hatred towards anyone and is a friend to all beings (Chapter 12, Verse 13).
- *Compassionate (Karuna):* They are compassionate and sympathetic towards others, sharing in their joys and sorrows (Chapter 12, Verse 13).
- *Forgiving (Kshama):* A *bhakta* is forgiving and tolerant, overlooking the faults and shortcomings of others (Chapter 12, Verse 13).
- *Contentment (Santushtah):* Content with whatever comes their way, a *bhakta* remains satisfied and does not crave material possessions (Chapter 12, Verse 14).
- *Self-control (Yatatma):* They exercise self-discipline and control over their senses and mind (Chapter 12, Verse 14).
- *Firm in Resolve (Dridha Nishchaya):* A *bhakta* has firm determination and unwavering faith in their spiritual path and practices (Chapter 12, Verse 14).
- *Detached (Aniketa):* They live a life of detachment, not overly attached to their home or possessions, and remain mentally free (Chapter 12, Verse 19).
- *Steadfast (Sthira-Matih):* They possess a steady intellect and are not swayed by transient emotions or distractions (Chapter 12, Verse 19).
- *Loving the Divine (Bhaktiman):* Above all, a *bhakta* loves the divine with all their heart, dedicating their life and actions to God (Chapter 12, Verse 20).

The Narada Bhakti Sutra and the *Bhagavad Gita* both provide comprehensive descriptions of the qualities that define a true devotee. These qualities emphasize humility, compassion, non-attachment, inner joy, and unwavering faith in the divine. By embodying these attributes, a *bhakta* can progress on the path of devotion, leading to spiritual fulfilment and union with the divine. These timeless qualities continue to inspire and guide spiritual seekers around the world, offering a profound and practical blueprint for living a life of devotion and spiritual excellence.

c. *According to other Religious Texts*

The qualities of a devotee, or a spiritually dedicated individual, are emphasised across various religious texts. These qualities often highlight virtues such as love, compassion, humility, and unwavering faith. Here is a look at the qualities of a devotee according to other major religious texts:

▶ Christianity (The Bible)

Key Qualities of a Devotee:

- *Love (Agape):* Love for God and for fellow humans is central to Christian devotion. The Bible teaches to "love your neighbor as yourself" (Mark 12:31) and to "love one another as I have loved you" (John 13:34).
- *Humility:* Humility is highly valued in Christianity. Devotees are encouraged to be humble, recognising their dependence on God. "Humble yourselves before the Lord, and he will lift you up" (James 4:10).
- *Faith:* Faith in God is fundamental. A devotee believes in God's promises and trusts in His plan. "Now faith is confidence in what we hope for and assurance about what we do not see" (Hebrews 11:1).
- *Compassion and Mercy:* Showing compassion and mercy to others is a key aspect of devotion. "Be kind and compassionate to one another, forgiving each other, just as in Christ God forgave you" (Ephesians 4:32).
- *Obedience:* Obedience to God's commandments is a sign of true devotion. "If you love me, keep my commands" (John 14:15).
- *Patience and Perseverance:* Devotees are called to be patient and to persevere in faith. "Be joyful in hope, patient in affliction, faithful in prayer" (Romans 12:12).
- *Holiness:* Striving to live a holy life, set apart for God, is essential. "But just as he who called you is holy, so be holy in all you do" (1 Peter 1:15).

▶ Islam (The Quran and Hadith)

Key Qualities of a Devotee (Mu'min):

- *Taqwa (God-consciousness):* A devotee is always aware of God's presence and strives to live righteously. "O you who have believed, fear Allah as He should be feared" (Quran 3:102).
- *Sabr (Patience):* Patience is highly valued. Devotees are encouraged to be steadfast in the face of trials. "Indeed, Allah is with the patient" (Quran 2:153).
- *Gratitude (Shukr):* Expressing gratitude to God for all blessings is a sign of devotion. "If you are grateful, I will surely increase you [in favor]" (Quran 14:7).

- *Compassion and Mercy (Rahma):* Being compassionate and merciful towards others is crucial. "And My mercy encompasses all things" (Quran 7:156).
- *Honesty and Integrity:* A true devotee is honest and maintains integrity. "O you who have believed, fear Allah and be with those who are true" (Quran 9:119).
- *Humility:* Humility is emphasised, recognising human limitations before God. "And the servants of the Most Merciful are those who walk upon the earth easily" (Quran 25:63).
- *Charity (Sadaqah):* Regularly giving in charity is a mark of devotion. "The example of those who spend their wealth in the way of Allah is like a seed [of grain] that sprouts seven ears" (Quran 2:261).

▸ Judaism (*The Torah and Talmud*)

Key Qualities of a Devotee:

- *Love of God:* Loving God with all one's heart, soul, and might is fundamental. "You shall love the Lord your God with all your heart and with all your soul and with all your might" (Deuteronomy 6:5).
- *Justice and Righteousness:* Pursuing justice and living righteously are essential. "But let justice roll down like waters, and righteousness like an ever-flowing stream" (Amos 5:24).
- *Humility:* Humility before God and others is crucial. "What does the Lord require of you but to do justice, and to love kindness, and to walk humbly with your God?" (Micah 6:8).
- *Compassion (Chesed):* Showing loving-kindness and compassion is a key virtue. "Do not seek revenge or bear a grudge against anyone among your people, but love your neighbour as yourself" (Leviticus 19:18).
- *Faithfulness:* Being faithful to God's commandments is a sign of devotion. "Keep my decrees and laws, for the person who obeys them will live by them" (Leviticus 18:5).
- *Patience and Endurance:* Patience and endurance, especially during trials, are valued. "Those who sow with tears will reap with songs of joy" (Psalm 126:5).
- *Gratitude:* Expressing gratitude to God is a daily practice. "Give thanks to the Lord, for he is good; his love endures forever" (Psalm 136:1).

▸ Buddhism (The Dhammapada and Sutras)

Key Qualities of a Devotee (*Upāsaka/Upāsikā*):

- *Loving-kindness (Metta):* Practicing loving-kindness towards all beings. "Let none through anger or ill-will wish harm upon another" (Dhammapada 1.5).

- *Compassion (Karuna):* Showing compassion and a desire to alleviate the suffering of others. "He who has no thought of 'I' and 'mine' whatever towards his mind and body, he who grieves not for that which he has not, he is indeed called a *Bhikkhu*" *(Dhammapada 367).*
- *Joy in Others' Happiness (Mudita):* Rejoicing in the happiness and success of others. "Cultivate a boundless heart towards all beings. Let your thoughts of boundless love pervade the whole world" (*Metta Sutta*).
- *Equanimity (Upekkha):* Maintaining calm and equanimity amidst the ups and downs of life is essential. "He who is calm in the midst of praise and blame, who is not shaken by the world and who is free from fear, he is called a sage" (*Dhammapada 81*).
- *Wisdom (Panna):* Cultivating wisdom and understanding the true nature of reality is crucial. "Better than a thousand hollow words, is one word that brings peace" (*Dhammapada 100*).
- *Ethical Conduct (Sila):* Adhering to ethical principles and living a moral life is important. "He who keeps not to his moral precepts, is unrestrained in conduct and habit, is unrefined and impure, such a one is not esteemed here and hereafter" (*Dhammapada 311*).
- *Mindfulness (Sati):* Practicing mindfulness and awareness in all activities is key. "Mindfulness is the path to the Deathless, unmindfulness is the path to death. Those who are mindful do not die, those who are not mindful are as if dead already" (*Dhammapada 21*).

Across different religious traditions, the qualities of a devotee are remarkably similar, emphasising virtues such as love, compassion, humility, patience, and unwavering faith. These qualities not only foster personal spiritual growth but also contribute to a more harmonious and compassionate society. By embodying these virtues, devotees across various faiths strive to live lives that are aligned with divine principles, ultimately seeking to unite with the higher power they revere.

Benefits and Practical Examples of Bhakti Yoga

Applied Bhakti Yoga refers to the practical application of Bhakti Yoga principles and practices in daily life to attain spiritual growth, emotional well-being, and a deeper connection with the divine. Bhakti Yoga itself is one of the traditional paths of yoga described in Hindu philosophy, focusing on devotion and love towards a personal aspect of the divine, whether it's a deity, guru, or a universal form of God.

Benefits of Applied Bhakti Yoga

- *Integration of Spirituality and Daily Life:* Integrates spiritual practices seamlessly into everyday activities, promoting a holistic approach to living.
- *Practical Devotional Practices:* Applied Bhakti Yoga involves engaging in practical devotional practices such as singing *bhajans* (devotional songs), chanting mantras, performing rituals (*puja*), and offering prayers. These practices help cultivate a loving and intimate relationship with the divine.
- *Integration into Daily Life:* Unlike some forms of yoga that are primarily practiced on the mat or during specific sessions, Applied Bhakti Yoga encourages devotees to integrate their devotional practices into all aspects of daily life. This includes maintaining an attitude of gratitude, offering selfless service (*seva*) to others, and seeing the divine presence in all beings.
- *Emotional Healing and Well-being:* Applied Bhakti Yoga is known for its profound emotional healing effects. By surrendering one's ego and desires to the divine, practitioners experience inner peace, contentment, and emotional stability. The practice helps in overcoming negative emotions such as anger, jealousy, and fear, replacing them with love and compassion.
- *Community and Social Harmony:* Devotees of Applied Bhakti Yoga often come together in spiritual communities (*satsang*) to share devotional practices, study scriptures, and support each other on their spiritual journeys. This fosters a sense of unity, compassion, and social harmony among practitioners.
- *Service to Humanity:* A significant aspect of Applied Bhakti Yoga is selfless service (*seva*) to humanity. Devotees engage in charitable activities, volunteering, and helping those in need as an expression of their devotion and love for the divine present in every living being.
- *Personal Transformation:* Through consistent practice, Applied Bhakti Yoga leads to personal transformation and spiritual growth. Devotees develop virtues such as humility, patience, forgiveness, and resilience, which are essential for navigating life's challenges with grace and equanimity.

Practical Examples of Applied Bhakti Yoga

- *Daily Prayer and Meditation:* Starting and ending the day with prayers and meditation focused on expressing gratitude and seeking guidance from the divine.

- *Chanting and Singing:* Regular practice of chanting mantras or singing devotional songs to invoke the presence of the divine and purify the mind.
- *Acting with Love and Compassion:* Treating others with kindness, empathy, and respect, seeing the divine presence in every person.
- *Engaging in Seva (Selfless Service):* Volunteering time and resources to help others in need, motivated by a sense of duty and devotion to the divine.

In essence, Applied Bhakti Yoga is about embodying the principles of devotion, love, and surrender in practical ways that enhance both individual well-being and collective harmony. It offers a transformative path for anyone seeking deeper spiritual connection and fulfilment in today's world.

Gyana (Jnana) Yoga in the Modern Era

Gyan Yoga, also known as Jnana Yoga, is one of the traditional paths of spiritual practice outlined in Hindu philosophy, particularly in the teachings of the *Bhagavad Gita* and other ancient scriptures. It focuses on the path of knowledge and wisdom as a means to spiritual realisation and liberation (moksha). In the modern era, the relevance and application of Gyan Yoga remain profound and significant, offering a timeless approach to spiritual growth amidst contemporary challenges. Here's a detailed exploration of its relevance and application.

Relevance of Gyan Yoga in the Modern Era

Quest for Truth and Understanding: In today's world, there is a widespread thirst for understanding the deeper truths of existence, beyond materialism and superficiality. Gyan Yoga provides a systematic framework for seekers to inquire into the nature of reality, consciousness, and the self.

- *Intellectual Exploration:* Gyan Yoga appeals to the intellectual mind, encouraging critical thinking, analysis, and contemplation. It invites individuals to explore philosophical concepts, metaphysics, and the profound wisdom embedded in ancient texts.
- *Integration with Science and Philosophy:* Gyan Yoga bridges the gap between spiritual wisdom and modern scientific inquiry. It offers insights that complement scientific discoveries, fostering a holistic understanding of the universe and human existence.

- *Inner Transformation:* The practice of Gyan Yoga involves self-inquiry and introspection, leading to inner transformation and personal growth. It helps individuals to transcend limiting beliefs, ego-driven desires, and attachments, promoting inner peace and harmony.
- *Development of Discernment:* In a world inundated with information and conflicting viewpoints, Gyan Yoga cultivates discernment (*viveka*) and clarity of thought. Practitioners learn to distinguish between truth and illusion, wisdom and ignorance.
- *Universal Application:* Unlike some paths of yoga that may require specific physical or ritualistic practices, Gyan Yoga can be practiced by anyone, regardless of age, gender, or cultural background. It transcends religious boundaries and is accessible to seekers of diverse beliefs.

Application of Gyan Yoga in Modern Life

Study of Sacred Texts: Engaging in the study of scriptures such as the *Bhagavad Gita*, *Upanishads*, and other philosophical texts forms a central practice of Gyan Yoga. This study deepens understanding and provides spiritual guidance.

- *Reflective Meditation:* Gyan Yoga encourages meditative practices focused on contemplation and reflection. Meditating on philosophical truths and profound questions helps in gaining insight into the nature of reality and the self.
- *Philosophical Inquiry and Dialogues:* Participating in philosophical discussions, dialogues, and debates fosters intellectual growth and enhances one's understanding of spiritual principles. It encourages an open-minded exploration of different perspectives.
- *Application in Professional and Personal Life:* The principles of Gyan Yoga, such as detachment (*vairagya*), equanimity (*samatvam*), and wisdom (*jnana*), can be applied in professional settings to promote ethical conduct, leadership qualities, and decision-making based on deeper understanding rather than mere emotions or desires.
- *Integration with Other Yogic Paths:* Gyan Yoga complements other paths of yoga, such as Bhakti Yoga (devotion), Karma Yoga (selfless action), and Raja Yoga (meditation and self-control). It provides a philosophical foundation and intellectual clarity that supports spiritual practice in these paths.

Benefits of Practicing Gyan Yoga

Intellectual Stimulation: Stimulates the intellect and enhances cognitive abilities through deep philosophical inquiry and study.

- *Clarity of Purpose:* Provides clarity of purpose and direction in life by illuminating the ultimate goal of spiritual realization.
- *Inner Peace and Contentment:* Leads to inner peace and contentment through understanding the transient nature of worldly pursuits and identifying with the eternal self.
- *Harmonious Relationships:* Facilitates harmonious relationships by fostering empathy, understanding, and wisdom in interactions with others.
- *Spiritual Fulfillment:* Ultimately leads to spiritual fulfilment and liberation (moksha) by transcending the limitations of the ego and realising the true nature of the self.

Gyan Yoga remains profoundly relevant in the modern era as it addresses the universal quest for knowledge, wisdom, and spiritual realisation. Its application in daily life fosters intellectual growth, inner transformation, and a deeper understanding of oneself and the universe. By integrating the principles of Gyan Yoga, individuals can navigate the complexities of contemporary life with greater clarity, purpose, and spiritual fulfilment.

Quality of a Gyana Yogi

The qualities of a *Gyana* Yogi, or a practitioner of Gyana Yoga (Jnana Yoga), are deeply rooted in the pursuit of knowledge, wisdom, and spiritual realisation. These qualities reflect the inner virtues and characteristics that enable individuals to engage effectively in the path of Gyana Yoga and advance towards spiritual enlightenment. Here are the essential qualities of a *Gyana* Yogi:

- *Intellectual Curiosity and Openness:* A *Gyana* Yogi possesses a strong intellectual curiosity and a deep thirst for knowledge. They are open-minded and eager to explore philosophical truths and spiritual teachings from various perspectives.
- *Discernment (Viveka):* Discernment is the ability to distinguish between the transient and the eternal, the real and the unreal. A *Gyana* Yogi cultivates keen discernment to navigate through the complexities of life and spiritual teachings.

- *Rational Thinking and Critical Analysis:* Gyana Yoga emphasizes rational thinking, logical reasoning, and critical analysis of concepts and beliefs. A *Gyana* Yogi employs these faculties to understand scriptures, philosophical texts, and the nature of reality.
- *Humility and Detachment:* Humility is essential in the practice of Gyana Yoga, as it helps the practitioner remain open to learning and guidance. Detachment from ego-based desires and attachments allows the *Gyana* Yogi to focus on higher spiritual pursuits.
- *Love for Truth (Satya):* The pursuit of truth (Satya) is central to Gyana Yoga. A *Gyana* Yogi is dedicated to uncovering the truth about the self, existence, and the ultimate reality through sincere inquiry and contemplation.
- *Inner Silence and Stillness:* Cultivating inner silence and stillness through meditation and introspection is crucial for a *Gyana* Yogi. This inner quietude allows for deeper insights and direct experiences of spiritual truths.
- *Integration of Knowledge and Practice:* Knowledge gained through study and reflection is integrated into daily life and spiritual practice. A *Gyana* Yogi strives to live in alignment with their understanding of spiritual truths and principles.
- *Patience and Perseverance:* Gyana Yoga is a path that requires patience and perseverance. The *Gyana* Yogi persists in their quest for knowledge and spiritual realisation, overcoming obstacles and challenges along the way.
- *Compassion and Universal Love:* While Gyana Yoga primarily focuses on knowledge and wisdom, a *Gyana* Yogi also embodies compassion and universal love. They recognise the interconnectedness of all beings and strive to alleviate suffering wherever possible.
- *Spiritual Humility and Service:* Spiritual humility involves recognizing the limitations of intellectual knowledge and surrendering to the divine wisdom. A *Gyana* Yogi may engage in selfless service (*seva*) as an expression of devotion and gratitude towards the divine.

The qualities of a *Gyana* Yogi encompass intellectual acumen, discernment, humility, devotion to truth, inner stillness, and compassion. These qualities enable the practitioner to deepen their understanding of spiritual truths, progress on the path of Gyana Yoga, and ultimately attain spiritual liberation (*moksha*) through knowledge and wisdom.

Karma Yoga (Yoga for Thoughtful-Action) in Modern Era

Karma Yoga, the yoga of selfless action, holds profound relevance and practical application in the modern era, offering a transformative path towards spiritual growth, ethical living, and societal harmony. Rooted in ancient Hindu philosophy and expounded in texts like the *Bhagavad Gita*, Karma Yoga emphasises performing actions selflessly, without attachment to outcomes, and with a sense of duty and service. Here's an exploration of its relevance and application in contemporary times:

Relevance of Karma Yoga in the Modern Era

Ethical Living and Responsibility: In a world facing complex ethical dilemmas and global challenges, Karma Yoga promotes ethical conduct and responsible action. It encourages individuals to perform their duties diligently, uphold moral values, and contribute positively to society.

- *Stress and Mental Well-being:* Modern lifestyles often lead to stress, anxiety, and burnout. Karma Yoga advocates working selflessly and without attachment to results, which reduces stress by shifting focus away from personal gains and towards service to others.
- *Social Justice and Service:* With growing disparities and social injustices, Karma Yoga inspires individuals to engage in selfless service (*seva*) and contribute towards social welfare. It fosters compassion, empathy, and a commitment to alleviating suffering in the community.
- *Work-Life Balance:* In the pursuit of success and material wealth, individuals often neglect their well-being and relationships. Karma Yoga promotes a balanced approach to work and life by encouraging mindful action, moderation, and detachment from excessive desires.
- *Environmental Sustainability:* Concerns about environmental degradation and climate change highlight the need for sustainable practices. Karma Yoga advocates responsible stewardship of the environment, promoting actions that benefit future generations and preserve natural resources.

Application of Karma Yoga in Modern Life

- Selfless Service (*Seva):* Practicing Karma Yoga involves engaging in selfless service for the welfare of others and society. This could range from volunteering at community centers, participating in environmental clean-ups, to supporting charitable organizations.

- *Workplace Ethics and Leadership:* Karma Yoga guides professionals to perform their duties with integrity, fairness, and dedication. Leaders practicing Karma Yoga prioritise the well-being of their teams and stakeholders, fostering a positive work culture.
- *Daily Activities with Awareness:* Karma Yoga encourages individuals to perform everyday tasks with mindfulness and awareness. Whether at home, work, or in social interactions, practicing Karma Yoga involves acting with sincerity, humility, and compassion.
- *Mindful Consumption and Sustainability:* Adopting Karma Yoga principles can influence consumer choices towards sustainability and ethical consumption. It involves mindful purchasing decisions, reducing waste, and supporting businesses that prioritise social and environmental responsibility.
- *Conflict Resolution and Harmony:* In personal relationships and community settings, Karma Yoga promotes forgiveness, tolerance, and reconciliation. By focusing on the intention behind actions rather than outcomes, individuals can resolve conflicts peacefully and foster harmonious relationships.

Benefits of Practicing Karma Yoga

- *Inner Peace and Contentment:* Acting selflessly and without attachment to results cultivates inner peace and contentment, irrespective of external circumstances.
- *Enhanced Emotional Well-being:* By reducing self-centered desires and ego, Karma Yoga mitigates stress, anxiety, and emotional turmoil, promoting emotional resilience and well-being.
- *Personal Growth and Character Development:* Practicing Karma Yoga enhances virtues such as humility, compassion, and gratitude, fostering personal growth and spiritual evolution.
- *Social Contribution and Community Building:* Through selfless service and ethical actions, Karma Yoga contributes positively to societal welfare, promoting community cohesion and collective well-being.
- *Spiritual Evolution:* Ultimately, Karma Yoga leads to spiritual growth and liberation (*moksha*) by purifying the mind, cultivating virtues, and aligning actions with higher spiritual principles.

Karma Yoga remains highly relevant in the modern era as it addresses contemporary challenges while offering a transformative path towards ethical living, societal harmony, and spiritual fulfilment. Its application in daily life empowers individuals to contribute positively to the world and attain inner peace through selfless service and mindful action.

Quality of a Karma Yogi

The qualities of a *Karma* Yogi, or a practitioner of Karma Yoga, are fundamental virtues and attitudes that guide their actions, mindset, and approach to life. These qualities enable the *Karma* Yogi to engage in selfless service, perform actions with dedication, and cultivate inner growth. Here are the essential qualities of a *Karma* Yogi:

- *Selflessness:* A *Karma* Yogi acts selflessly, without attachment to personal gain or recognition. They perform their duties and service with the intention of benefiting others or contributing to the greater good, rather than seeking personal gratification.
- *Detachment from Results:* Central to Karma Yoga is the principle of detachment (vairagya) from the outcomes of actions. A *Karma* Yogi remains equanimous, whether success or failure results from their efforts, understanding that they control actions, not results.
- *Dedication and Commitment:* Karma Yoga emphasises dedication and commitment to one's duties and responsibilities. A *Karma* Yogi approaches tasks with sincerity, diligence, and perseverance, regardless of the challenges or obstacles encountered.
- *Integrity and Ethical Conduct:* Upholding moral values and ethical principles is essential for a *Karma* Yogi. They act with honesty, fairness, and integrity in all interactions, maintaining a high standard of ethical conduct both personally and professionally.
- *Mindfulness and Awareness:* Practicing mindfulness and awareness in every action is key for a *Karma* Yogi. They remain present and attentive, conscious of their thoughts, intentions, and the impact of their actions on others and the environment.
- *Humility and Service Orientation:* Humility is a hallmark of a *Karma* Yogi, as they recognise their interconnectedness with others and the universe. They serve others with humility, acknowledging the divine presence in all beings and treating everyone with respect and compassion.
- *Equanimity in Adversity:* Life brings challenges and uncertainties, and a *Karma* Yogi maintains inner balance and equanimity amidst adversity. They accept situations with grace, learning from experiences and using setbacks as opportunities for growth.
- *Compassion and Empathy:* Compassion towards others and empathy for their struggles are inherent qualities of a *Karma* Yogi.

They understand and alleviate the suffering of others through compassionate action and supportive presence.

- *Generosity and Sharing:* A *Karma* Yogi practices generosity by sharing their time, resources, and knowledge for the welfare of others. They give freely and willingly, without expecting anything in return, fostering a spirit of abundance and goodwill.
- *Spiritual Growth and Self-Reflection:* Continuous self-reflection and introspection are integral to the path of Karma Yoga. A *Karma* Yogi strives for spiritual growth, seeking to deepen their understanding of themselves, their purpose, and their connection to the divine.
- *Gratitude and Contentment:* Cultivating gratitude for blessings, opportunities, and challenges is essential for a *Karma* Yogi. They maintain a sense of contentment and appreciation for life's experiences, recognising each moment as an opportunity for spiritual evolution.
- *Service to Humanity:* Above all, a *Karma* Yogi dedicates their life to service to humanity and the world. They actively contribute to social welfare, environmental sustainability, and community building, embodying the principle of "*Loka Samasta Sukhino Bhavantu*" – May all beings be happy.

The qualities of a *Karma* Yogi encompass selflessness, detachment from outcomes, dedication, integrity, mindfulness, humility, equanimity, compassion, generosity, spiritual growth, gratitude, and service to humanity. These qualities guide their actions, inspire others, and contribute to creating a more harmonious and compassionate world.

Raja Yoga (Yoga of Mind) in the Modern Era

Raja Yoga, often referred to as the "Royal Path" or the "Yoga of Mind," is a comprehensive system of spiritual practice outlined in ancient Hindu philosophy, particularly expounded in texts like the Yoga Sutras of Patanjali. It focuses on the cultivation of mental discipline, concentration, meditation, and ultimately, the realisation of the self. In the modern era, Raja Yoga remains profoundly relevant and offers practical applications that resonate with contemporary challenges and aspirations. Here's an exploration of its relevance and application:

Relevance of Raja Yoga in the Modern Era

- *Stress Reduction and Mental Well-being:* In today's fast-paced and hectic lifestyles, stress and mental health issues are prevalent.

Raja Yoga offers techniques such as meditation (*dhyana*), breath control (*pranayama*), and mental concentration (*dharana*) to calm the mind, reduce stress, and enhance emotional resilience.

- *Enhanced Cognitive Abilities:* Raja Yoga practices improve cognitive functions such as focus, memory, and clarity of thought. In professions requiring high mental acuity, such as education, research, and technology, Raja Yoga techniques can significantly boost productivity and creativity.
- *Mind-Body Connection:* Raja Yoga emphasises the integration of mind and body through practices like *asanas* (postures) and *pranayama*. These practices promote physical health, flexibility, and overall well-being, aligning with holistic health approaches increasingly valued in modern healthcare.
- *Self-awareness and Emotional Intelligence:* Through self-observation and introspection, Raja Yoga cultivates self-awareness and emotional intelligence. Practitioners learn to manage emotions, develop empathy, and foster harmonious relationships in personal and professional life.
- *Spiritual Growth and Inner Transformation:* Raja Yoga leads to spiritual growth and self-realisation by transcending the limitations of the ego and connecting with the higher self. It offers a systematic path for seekers to explore the nature of consciousness, existence, and the ultimate reality.

Application of Raja Yoga in Modern Life

- *Meditation and Mindfulness Practices:* Meditation techniques taught in Raja Yoga, such as mindfulness meditation and mantra meditation, are widely adopted in secular settings for stress reduction, mental clarity, and emotional well-being.
- *Corporate Wellness Programs:* Many organisations incorporate Raja Yoga practices into their wellness programs to improve employee morale, productivity, and overall health. Techniques like meditation and stress management workshops enhance workplace satisfaction and reduce absenteeism.
- *Educational Settings:* Schools and universities integrate Raja Yoga techniques to enhance students' concentration, academic performance, and emotional resilience. Practices such as mindfulness and breath awareness support learning environments conducive to focus and creativity.
- *Healthcare and Therapy:* Raja Yoga practices complement traditional healthcare approaches by promoting relaxation, reducing

chronic pain, and supporting mental health treatment. Integrative medicine clinics often incorporate yoga therapy to address physical and psychological ailments.

- *Personal Development and Leadership:* Raja Yoga fosters personal development by enhancing self-discipline, clarity of thought, and decision-making abilities. Leaders practicing Raja Yoga exhibit qualities such as calmness, empathy, and vision, inspiring others through their balanced approach.

Benefits of Practicing Raja Yoga

- *Stress Reduction and Relaxation:* Techniques like meditation and *pranayama* alleviate stress, promote relaxation, and improve overall mental and physical health.
- *Improved Concentration and Focus:* Raja Yoga practices enhance concentration, memory retention, and cognitive abilities, supporting academic and professional success.
- *Emotional Resilience and Well-being:* Cultivating mindfulness and self-awareness leads to emotional stability, resilience, and enhanced interpersonal relationships.
- *Spiritual Awareness and Self-realisation:* Raja Yoga facilitates spiritual growth, self-discovery, and realization of one's true nature beyond the ego, fostering inner peace and fulfilment.
- *Holistic Health Benefits:* The integration of mind-body practices in Raja Yoga supports holistic health, promoting vitality, flexibility, and longevity.

Raja Yoga remains highly relevant in the modern era as it addresses the holistic well-being of individuals and society. Its practical applications in diverse fields contribute to personal growth, professional success, and spiritual evolution, making it a valuable path for navigating the complexities of contemporary life with mindfulness, wisdom, and inner peace.

Quality of a Raja Yogi in the Modern Era

In the modern era, a *Raja* Yogi, or practitioner of Raja Yoga, embodies qualities that facilitate spiritual growth, mental clarity, and harmonious living amidst the complexities of contemporary life. Here are the essential qualities of a *Raja* Yogi:

- *Discipline (Tapas):* Raja Yoga emphasises discipline in thoughts, actions, and lifestyle. A *Raja* Yogi practices self-control, punctuality, and dedication to spiritual practices like meditation and self-reflection.

- *Concentration* (*Dharana*): Central to Raja Yoga is the ability to focus the mind intensely on a single point or object. A *Raja* Yogi cultivates concentration through practices such as breath awareness, mantra repetition, or visualisation.
- *Mental Equanimity* (*Samatvam*): In the face of success or failure, praise or criticism, a *Raja* Yogi maintains mental equilibrium. They remain calm, composed, and unaffected by external circumstances, cultivating inner stability and resilience.
- *Self-awareness (Svadhyaya):* Self-study and introspection are vital for a *Raja* Yogi. They reflect on their thoughts, emotions, and behaviors to gain deeper self-awareness and understanding of their spiritual journey.
- *Detachment (Vairagya):* A *Raja* Yogi practices detachment from material possessions, ego-based desires, and transient pleasures. They seek contentment and fulfillment within, rather than relying on external factors for happiness.
- *Humility (Vinaya):* Humility is a hallmark of spiritual maturity in Raja Yoga. A *Raja* Yogi remains modest, acknowledging their limitations, and respects the inherent divinity in all beings.
- *Integrity (Satya):* Truthfulness and honesty are essential for a *Raja* Yogi. They align their thoughts, words, and actions with higher moral and ethical principles, fostering trust and authenticity in relationships.
- *Compassion (Karuna):* Compassion towards oneself and others is integral to Raja Yoga. A *Raja* Yogi cultivates empathy, kindness, and a willingness to alleviate the suffering of all beings.
- *Patience (Dhriti):* Spiritual progress in Raja Yoga requires patience and perseverance. A *Raja* Yogi patiently engages in daily practices, trusting in the gradual unfoldment of wisdom and inner transformation.
- *Service (Seva)*: Serving others selflessly is a natural expression of a *Raja* Yogi's spiritual journey. They contribute to the welfare of society, offering their skills, knowledge, and resources for the benefit of others without expecting recognition or reward.
- *Open-mindedness and Adaptability:* In a rapidly changing world, a *Raja* Yogi remains open-minded and adaptable. They embrace new ideas, perspectives, and experiences that contribute to their spiritual growth and understanding.

- Spiritual Aspiration (*Utsaha):* A *Raja* Yogi harbors a fervent aspiration for spiritual realisation and self-transcendence. They diligently pursue higher states of consciousness and strive for union with the divine within.

In essence, the qualities of a *Raja* Yogi encompass discipline, concentration, mental equanimity, self-awareness, detachment, humility, integrity, compassion, patience, service, open-mindedness, and spiritual aspiration. These qualities guide their spiritual practices, interactions with others, and contribute to creating a more harmonious and enlightened society in the modern era.

Hatha Yoga (Yoga For Body and Mind) in the Modern Era

Hatha Yoga, often recognised as the yoga of physical postures (*asanas*) and breath control (*pranayama*), holds significant relevance and practical application in the modern era. Originating from ancient Hindu traditions and later integrated into various global wellness practices, Hatha Yoga offers a holistic approach to cultivating physical health, mental well-being, and spiritual harmony. Here's an exploration of its relevance and application in contemporary times:

Relevance of Hatha Yoga in the Modern Era

- *Physical Health and Fitness:* In an era marked by sedentary lifestyles and rising health concerns, Hatha Yoga provides a comprehensive system of physical exercise. It improves flexibility, strength, balance, and overall fitness through a variety of yoga postures (*asanas*) and sequences.
- *Stress Reduction and Relaxation:* Modern life often leads to stress, anxiety, and mental fatigue. Hatha Yoga incorporates relaxation techniques, deep breathing exercises (*pranayama*), and meditation to calm the mind, reduce stress hormones, and promote emotional well-being.
- *Mind-Body Connection:* Hatha Yoga emphasises the integration of mind and body through conscious movement and breath awareness. Practicing yoga postures enhances body awareness, mindfulness, and the ability to manage emotions and sensations.
- *Holistic Wellness:* Beyond physical fitness, Hatha Yoga addresses holistic wellness by balancing energy (*prana*) flow within the body. Techniques such as *pranayama* regulate breathing patterns, improve oxygenation, and support overall health and vitality.

- *Therapeutic Benefits:* Hatha Yoga is increasingly recognised in healthcare settings for its therapeutic benefits. It complements medical treatments for conditions such as chronic pain, hypertension, insomnia, and depression, promoting healing and rehabilitation.

Application of Hatha Yoga in Modern Life

- *Yoga Studios and Classes:* Hatha Yoga classes are widely accessible in yoga studios, fitness centers, and online platforms. They cater to individuals of all ages and fitness levels, offering structured sessions that include *asanas*, *pranayama*, and relaxation techniques.
- *Corporate Wellness Programs:* Many workplaces integrate Hatha Yoga into employee wellness programs to improve productivity, reduce absenteeism, and enhance overall job satisfaction. Yoga sessions promote stress management and foster a positive work environment.
- *Sports and Athletic Training:* Athletes and sports enthusiasts incorporate Hatha Yoga to enhance flexibility, prevent injuries, and improve performance. Yoga postures complement strength training and conditioning exercises, supporting optimal physical fitness.
- *Medical and Rehabilitation Settings:* Healthcare providers recommend Hatha Yoga as part of integrative medicine approaches. Yoga therapy sessions are tailored to address specific health concerns, providing gentle yet effective rehabilitation for musculoskeletal disorders and chronic illnesses.
- *Personal Wellness Practices:* Individuals practice Hatha Yoga as part of their daily routine for personal well-being and self-care. Morning or evening yoga sessions help maintain physical fitness, reduce stress levels, and promote relaxation after a busy day.

Benefits of Practicing Hatha Yoga

- *Improved Physical Flexibility and Strength:* Regular practice of yoga postures enhances flexibility, increases muscle tone, and improves joint mobility.
- *Stress Reduction and Emotional Balance:* Hatha Yoga techniques such as deep breathing and relaxation promote relaxation, reduce cortisol levels, and enhance emotional resilience.
- *Enhanced Pulmonary Function: Pranayama* exercises improve lung capacity, oxygen uptake, and respiratory efficiency, supporting overall cardiovascular health.

- *Mental Clarity and Focus:* Yoga practices cultivate mindfulness, concentration, and mental clarity, improving cognitive function and decision-making abilities.
- *Spiritual Awareness and Self-discovery:* Hatha Yoga serves as a gateway to deeper self-awareness, spiritual growth, and connection with inner peace and higher consciousness.

Hatha Yoga remains highly relevant in the modern era for its holistic approach to physical health, mental well-being, and spiritual development. Its practical applications in diverse settings contribute to promoting overall wellness, stress management, and personal transformation, making it a valuable practice for individuals seeking balance and harmony in their lives.

Quality of a Hatha Yogi in the Modern Era

In the modern era, a *Hatha* Yogi embodies qualities that support physical health, mental well-being, and spiritual growth through the practice of yoga postures (*asanas*), breath control (*pranayama*), and other techniques. These qualities enable the practitioner to cultivate a balanced lifestyle, promote inner harmony, and contribute positively to their community. Here are the essential qualities of a *Hatha* Yogi in the modern era:

- *Commitment to Practice:* A *Hatha* Yogi demonstrates dedication and consistency in their yoga practice. They prioritise regularity in attending classes, engaging in personal practice, and exploring various aspects of Hatha Yoga to deepen their understanding and proficiency.
- *Mindfulness and Presence:* Practicing mindfulness both on and off the yoga mat is crucial for a *Hatha* Yogi. They cultivate present-moment awareness during yoga sessions, daily activities, and interactions with others, fostering a deeper connection with themselves and their surroundings.
- *Physical Discipline and Body Awareness:* Hatha Yoga emphasises physical discipline through the precise alignment and execution of yoga postures. A *Hatha* Yogi develops keen body awareness, enhancing flexibility, strength, and balance while preventing injuries through mindful movement.
- *Breath Awareness and Pranayama:* Mastery of breath control (*pranayama*) is fundamental in Hatha Yoga. A Hatha Yogi practices various *pranayama* techniques to regulate breathing patterns, increase energy flow (prana), and promote relaxation and mental clarity.

- *Adaptability and Openness:* In a dynamic and diverse world, a *Hatha* Yogi remains adaptable and open to learning. They embrace different yoga styles, teachings, and perspectives, integrating beneficial practices into their personal journey without attachment to rigid dogma.
- *Patience and Persistence:* Progress in Hatha Yoga requires patience and persistence. A Hatha Yogi approaches challenges with resilience, understanding that growth and transformation unfold gradually through consistent effort and dedication.
- *Self-care and Wellness:* Beyond physical fitness, a *Hatha* Yogi prioritizes holistic self-care and well-being. They adopt a balanced diet, adequate rest, and mindful lifestyle habits that complement their yoga practice, nurturing overall health and vitality.
- *Humility and Respect:* Humility is a hallmark of spiritual maturity in Hatha Yoga. A Hatha Yogi respects their teachers, fellow practitioners, and the lineage of yoga, embodying humility in their journey of self-discovery and personal growth.
- *Compassion and Service:* Compassion towards oneself and others is integral to the practice of Hatha Yoga. A Hatha Yogi extends kindness, empathy, and support to others, fostering a sense of community and contributing positively to society through acts of service (*seva*).
- *Integrity and Ethical Conduct:* Upholding ethical principles and integrity is essential for a *Hatha* Yogi. They demonstrate honesty, fairness, and accountability in all interactions, reflecting the moral values and teachings of yoga in their daily life.
- *Spiritual Inquiry and Self-realisation:* Hatha Yoga serves as a pathway to spiritual inquiry and self-realisation. A Hatha Yogi explores the deeper dimensions of consciousness, seeking to transcend egoic limitations and experience union with the divine within.
- *Gratitude and Contentment:* Cultivating gratitude for life's blessings and experiences is vital for a *Hatha* Yogi. They embrace each moment with appreciation and contentment, recognising yoga as a transformative practice that enriches their existence.

The qualities of a *Hatha* Yogi in the modern era encompass commitment to practice, mindfulness, physical discipline, breath awareness, adaptability, patience, self-care, humility, compassion, integrity, spiritual inquiry, and gratitude. These qualities guide their journey of self-discovery, enhance well-being, and inspire others through the transformative power of Hatha Yoga.

3

Yoga in Education
School, College and University

Yoga has transcended its ancient roots in spiritual practice to become a widely recognised and valued discipline in modern educational settings, spanning schools, colleges, and universities worldwide. Originally developed thousands of years ago in India as a holistic system for physical, mental, and spiritual well-being, yoga has evolved into a versatile tool that enhances academic performance, fosters emotional resilience, and cultivates overall health among students of all ages.

Evolution of Yoga in Education

In recent decades, there has been a notable shift towards integrating yoga into educational curricula, driven by growing awareness of its manifold benefits. Initially embraced for its physical health benefits such as improved flexibility, strength, and posture, yoga's influence has expanded to encompass its profound effects on mental clarity, emotional regulation, and stress reduction.

The integration of yoga into education represents a significant evolution in educational practices globally, extending from schools to colleges and universities. What began as a traditional practice rooted in ancient Indian philosophy has evolved into a recognised tool for promoting physical health, mental well-being, and overall academic success among students of all ages.

Ancient Roots and Philosophical Foundations

Yoga originated over 5,000 years ago in the Indus-Sarasvati civilisation of Northern India, with its philosophical roots embedded in texts such as the *Vedas*, *Upanishads*, and *Bhagavad Gita*. Initially, yoga was primarily a spiritual discipline aimed at achieving union with the divine through physical postures (*asanas*), breath control (*pranayama*), and meditation.

Early Adoption in Educational Settings

The adoption of yoga in educational settings began in India, where it was traditionally taught in gurukuls (ancient schools) as part of a holistic education that included moral, intellectual, and physical development. Students learned yoga alongside academic subjects to cultivate discipline, concentration, and inner awareness.

Global Spread and Popularity

In the 20th and 21st centuries, yoga's popularity surged globally, driven by its proven benefits for physical health and mental well-being. As scientific research validated yoga's efficacy in reducing stress, improving focus, and enhancing emotional regulation, educators worldwide began integrating yoga into school curricula.

Yoga in Schools

In schools, yoga programmes are designed to support students' physical fitness, mental clarity, and emotional resilience. Through structured yoga classes, students learn mindfulness techniques, relaxation exercises, and gentle yoga postures tailored to their age and developmental stage. These practices help reduce anxiety, enhance concentration, and promote a positive classroom atmosphere conducive to learning.

Yoga in Higher Education

At the collegiate level, universities have embraced yoga as part of comprehensive wellness programmes aimed at supporting students' overall health and academic success. Yoga classes and workshops are offered to help students manage stress, improve sleep quality, and maintain physical fitness amidst the demands of higher education.

Research and Evidence-Based Practice

Scientific research continues to validate the benefits of yoga in educational settings, highlighting its role in improving cognitive function, enhancing academic performance, and fostering social-emotional learning. Studies show that regular yoga practice can boost memory retention, increase attention span, and cultivate resilience in students facing academic challenges.

Integration into Modern Educational Philosophy

The evolution of yoga in education reflects a broader shift towards holistic education models that prioritise students' physical, mental, and emotional well-being. Educators recognise yoga as a transformative tool for cultivating life skills such as self-discipline, empathy, and mindfulness, essential for personal growth and future success.

The evolution of yoga in education signifies a progressive integration of ancient wisdom with modern educational practices. As schools, colleges, and universities worldwide continue to embrace yoga, its role in promoting student well-being, enhancing academic performance, and fostering a positive learning environment is poised to expand further. By incorporating yoga into education, educators are not only nurturing healthier, more resilient students but also laying the foundation for a more balanced and compassionate society.

Yoga's Impact on Student Well-being

In schools, yoga programs are increasingly valued for their ability to promote mindfulness and enhance concentration, crucial factors in academic success. By incorporating breathing exercises (*pranayama*), meditation techniques, and gentle physical postures (*asanas*), educators aim to provide students with practical tools to manage stress, anxiety, and peer pressure effectively.

Yoga has emerged as a powerful tool for enhancing student well-being in educational settings, offering a multitude of benefits that contribute to physical health, mental clarity, emotional resilience, and overall academic success. As schools, colleges, and universities integrate yoga into their curricula and wellness programs, its impact on student well-being becomes increasingly evident and profound.

Physical Health Benefits

- *Improved Flexibility and Strength:* Yoga postures (*asanas*) promote flexibility, strength, and muscle tone, helping students maintain a healthy and balanced body.
- *Enhanced Physical Fitness:* Regular practice of yoga contributes to cardiovascular health, stamina, and overall physical fitness levels, supporting students in maintaining optimal health.
- *Better Posture and Alignment:* Yoga helps correct postural imbalances caused by prolonged sitting, contributing to better spinal alignment and reducing the risk of musculoskeletal issues.

Mental Well-being Benefits

- *Stress Reduction:* Yoga techniques such as deep breathing (*pranayama*) and mindfulness meditation alleviate stress, calm the nervous system, and promote relaxation.

- *Improved Concentration and Focus:* Through mindfulness practices, students enhance their ability to concentrate, focus attention, and sustain mental clarity during academic tasks and examinations.
- *Emotional Regulation:* Yoga fosters emotional resilience by teaching students to manage emotions effectively, reducing anxiety, and promoting a positive outlook on challenges.

Psychological Benefits

- *Enhanced Cognitive Function:* Research indicates that yoga improves cognitive function, including memory retention, information processing speed, and decision-making abilities.
- *Better Sleep Quality:* Yoga promotes better sleep patterns, helping students achieve deeper and more restorative sleep, which is crucial for cognitive functioning and academic performance.
- *Mood Enhancement:* Regular yoga practice releases endorphins and boosts serotonin levels, enhancing mood, and promoting a sense of well-being among students.

Social and Behavioural Benefits

- *Improved Social Interaction:* Yoga fosters a sense of community and camaraderie among students participating in group yoga classes or workshops, promoting positive social interaction and teamwork.
- *Behavioural Management:* Yoga teaches self-discipline, self-control, and patience, which are essential for managing behaviour, reducing impulsivity, and promoting respectful communication.

Holistic Development

- *Self-awareness and Mindful Living:* Yoga encourages students to cultivate self-awareness, self-compassion, and acceptance, fostering a deeper understanding of themselves and their emotions.
- *Life Skills Development:* Beyond physical and mental benefits, yoga in stills life skills such as resilience, empathy, and mindfulness, preparing students for personal growth and future challenges.

Integrating Yoga into Educational Settings

Educators and administrators recognise the transformative impact of yoga on student well-being and academic success. Schools, colleges, and universities are increasingly incorporating yoga into their daily routines, physical education programmes, and wellness initiatives to create supportive learning environments that nurture the whole student.

Yoga's impact on student well-being extends far beyond physical exercise. It encompasses mental clarity, emotional resilience, and holistic development, empowering students to thrive academically and personally. By embracing yoga, educational institutions not only promote healthier lifestyles but also cultivate essential life skills that prepare students for success in a rapidly changing world. As the evidence of yoga's benefits continues to grow, its role in fostering student well-being remains pivotal in shaping the future of education.

Implementing Yoga in Colleges and Universities

At the collegiate level, yoga finds application as a holistic approach to student wellness. Universities worldwide offer yoga classes and workshops as part of their wellness programs, addressing the mental health challenges that often accompany rigorous academic demands. Yoga sessions help students unwind, improve sleep quality, and foster a balanced lifestyle conducive to optimal learning and personal growth.

Implementing yoga in colleges and universities has become increasingly popular as educational institutions recognise the profound benefits it offers to students' overall well-being and academic achievement & success. From enhancing physical fitness to promoting mental clarity and emotional resilience, yoga programs are being integrated into campuses worldwide to create supportive learning environments. Here's how yoga can be effectively implemented in colleges and universities:

Establishing Yoga Programmes at College/ University Level

- *Curricular Integration:* Introduce yoga as part of the physical education curriculum or elective courses. Offer classes that cater to different levels of experience, from beginners to advanced practitioners, ensuring inclusivity.
- *Wellness Initiatives:* Integrate yoga into comprehensive wellness programmes that address students' physical, mental, and emotional health. Offer workshops, seminars, and retreats focusing on yoga practices such as *asanas* (postures), *pranayama* (breathing exercises), and meditation.
- *Dedicated Yoga Spaces:* Designate dedicated yoga studios or multipurpose spaces equipped with yoga mats, props, and calming ambiance. Ensure these spaces are easily accessible and conducive to yoga practice.

Hiring Qualified Instructors

- *Certified Yoga Teachers:* Recruit certified yoga instructors who have experience working with college-age students. Look for instructors who can adapt yoga practices to meet the diverse needs and abilities of students.
- *Specialised Training:* Provide opportunities for instructors to receive specialised training in yoga for educational settings, including techniques for stress management, mindfulness, and adapting practices for academic schedules.

Promoting Student Engagement

- *Student Clubs and Organizations:* Support student-led yoga clubs or organisations that organise regular yoga sessions, events, and community outreach initiatives. Encourage leadership opportunities for students interested in promoting yoga on campus.
- *Inclusive Programming:* Offer yoga sessions that cater to specific student populations, such as athletes, international students, or those with disabilities. Ensure diversity and inclusivity in yoga offerings to meet the varying needs of the student body.

Integrating Yoga Across Disciplines

- *Interdisciplinary Approach:* Explore opportunities to integrate yoga principles and practices into other academic disciplines, such as psychology, health sciences, or philosophy. Foster dialogue and research on the intersection of yoga with academic and professional fields.
- *Faculty and Staff Participation:* Encourage faculty and staff to participate in yoga classes and workshops to promote a culture of wellness and mindfulness across the campus community. Offer incentives or wellness programmes to encourage participation.

Assessing Impact and Feedback

- *Evaluation and Feedback*: Implement mechanisms to gather feedback from students, faculty, and staff regarding their experiences with yoga programmes. Use surveys, focus groups, or assessments to evaluate the impact of yoga on student well-being, academic performance, and campus culture.
- *Continuous Improvement:* Use feedback and assessment data to refine and improve yoga programmes over time. Incorporate best practices, new research findings, and student preferences into program development and implementation.

Collaboration and Partnerships

- *Community Partnerships:* Collaborate with local yoga studios, wellness centres, or healthcare providers to offer specialised workshops, guest lectures, or joint programmes. Build partnerships that enrich the yoga offerings available to students and promote community engagement.
- *Alumni Engagement:* Engage alumni who have benefited from yoga programmes during their time on campus. Create opportunities for alumni to contribute back through mentorship, guest teaching, or financial support for yoga initiatives.

By implementing yoga programmes in colleges and universities, institutions can foster a culture of holistic well-being, resilience, and academic success among students. Yoga programmes provide valuable tools for stress management, physical fitness, and personal growth, preparing students to thrive in their academic pursuits and beyond. As yoga continues to evolve as a cornerstone of campus wellness initiatives, educational institutions play a vital role in promoting lifelong habits of health, mindfulness, and self-care among their student communities.

Academic and Cognitive Benefits

Research underscores the cognitive benefits of yoga, demonstrating improvements in memory retention, cognitive flexibility, and information processing speed among practitioners. These enhancements are particularly valuable in academic environments where critical thinking and academic performance are paramount.

Implementing yoga programmes at the college and university level has shown significant impact on academic and cognitive benefits among students. These programmes integrate yoga practices such as *asanas* (postures), *pranayama* (breathing exercises), and meditation into campus wellness initiatives, aiming to enhance overall student well-being and academic success. Here's a detailed exploration of the academic and cognitive benefits observed:

Academic Benefits

- *Improved Concentration and Focus:* Yoga practices, particularly mindfulness meditation and breath awareness techniques, help students improve their ability to concentrate during lectures, study sessions, and examinations. Enhanced focus leads to better retention of information and improved academic performance.

- *Enhanced Cognitive Function:* Research indicates that regular practice of yoga can enhance cognitive functions such as memory retention, information processing speed, and decision-making abilities. These cognitive enhancements are crucial for academic success across various disciplines.
- *Stress Reduction and Academic Anxiety:* Yoga programmes equip students with effective stress management tools, reducing levels of anxiety related to academic pressures and deadlines. Lower stress levels contribute to a more conducive learning environment and improved mental well-being.
- *Better Time Management and Organisation:* Through yoga practice, students develop skills in self-discipline, time management, and organisational strategies. These skills are instrumental in balancing academic responsibilities and extracurricular activities effectively.

Cognitive Benefits

- *Enhanced Mental Clarity and Alertness:* Yoga practices promote mental clarity, alertness, and heightened awareness of present-moment experiences. This mental clarity translates into improved problem-solving abilities and critical thinking skills among students.
- *Emotional Regulation and Resilience:* Yoga enhances emotional resilience by teaching students techniques to manage negative emotions, stress, and emotional fluctuations. Emotional regulation contributes to overall well-being and academic persistence.
- *Increased Brain Plasticity:* Regular yoga practice has been associated with increased brain plasticity, which refers to the brain's ability to adapt and reorganise neural pathways in response to learning and experience. This adaptability supports cognitive flexibility and creativity among students.
- *Better Sleep Quality:* Many students experience improved sleep quality as a result of participating in yoga programmes. Quality sleep is essential for cognitive function, memory consolidation, and overall academic performance.

Long-term Impact

- *Lifelong Habits of Wellness:* Engaging in yoga during college fosters lifelong habits of wellness, mindfulness, and self-care. Students are more likely to continue practicing yoga beyond their academic years, reaping long-term benefits for their physical health and mental well-being.

- *Preparation for Career Success:* The cognitive and emotional skills developed through yoga practice—such as resilience, focus, and stress management—are valuable assets in professional settings. Graduates equipped with these skills are better prepared for career success and leadership roles.

While we are not currently implementing yoga programmes at the college or university level, we are on the path of building a nation by fostering citizens with a sense of humanity and culture. Implementing yoga programmes at the college and university level yields profound academic and cognitive benefits for students. By enhancing concentration, cognitive function, emotional regulation, and overall well-being, yoga contributes to a positive learning environment conducive to academic success and personal growth. As educational institutions continue to recognise the holistic benefits of yoga, they play a pivotal role in promoting student well-being and preparing them for future challenges in academic and professional pursuits.

Beyond Physical Practice: Cultivating Life Skills

Moreover, yoga in education extends beyond the physical and cognitive domains to nurture essential life skills such as empathy, resilience, and self-discipline. Through guided mindfulness practices and ethical teachings rooted in yoga philosophy, students learn to navigate interpersonal relationships, cultivate a sense of responsibility, and develop a positive attitude towards learning and personal development.

As yoga continues to gain recognition as a transformative educational tool, its integration into schools, colleges, and universities reflects a broader paradigm shift towards holistic education. By fostering physical health, mental clarity, emotional resilience, and life skills development, yoga contributes significantly to creating nurturing educational environments that support the holistic well-being and academic success of students worldwide.

Relevance of Practicing Yoga in the Education

Practicing yoga in the education sector, encompassing schools, colleges, and universities, holds immense relevance in fostering holistic development, enhancing well-being, and promoting academic success among students. Here's a detailed exploration of the relevance of yoga in each educational setting:

School

- *Physical Health and Fitness*: Yoga promotes physical health through *asanas* (postures) that improve flexibility, strength, and overall fitness. Introducing yoga at a young age encourages healthy habits and addresses issues like poor posture or sedentary lifestyles among children.
- *Emotional Regulation:* School can be stressful for students due to academic pressures and social challenges. Yoga teaches children mindfulness techniques and relaxation exercises that enhance emotional regulation, reducing anxiety and promoting a positive school environment.
- *Improved Concentration and Academic Performance:* Yoga practices such as breathing exercises and meditation enhance concentration and focus. Students who practice yoga are better equipped to manage distractions in the classroom, leading to improved academic performance and retention of information.
- *Social and Emotional Learning:* Yoga fosters social-emotional skills like empathy, compassion, and resilience. These skills are crucial for developing positive relationships with peers and teachers, promoting a supportive and inclusive school community.

Colleges

- *Pressure Management:* College students face academic demands, peer pressure, and transitions to independence. Yoga helps students manage stress effectively, reducing cortisol levels and promoting mental clarity, which supports academic success.
- *Enhanced Mental Health:* Yoga programmes in colleges provide students with tools to cope with mental health challenges such as depression and anxiety. Regular practice improves mood, self-esteem, and overall psychological well-being.
- *Balanced Lifestyle:* College life often includes irregular schedules, unhealthy eating habits, and lack of exercise. Yoga encourages a balanced lifestyle by promoting mindful eating, adequate sleep, and physical activity, which are essential for academic and personal success.
- *Community Building:* Yoga classes and clubs create opportunities for students to connect with like-minded peers, fostering a sense

of belonging and camaraderie on campus. This community support network contributes to overall student satisfaction and engagement.

Universities

- *Comprehensive Wellness Programmes:* Universities integrate yoga into comprehensive wellness initiatives that prioritize student well-being. Yoga complements other health-promoting activities such as counselling services, fitness programs, and health education workshops.
- *Leadership and Career Readiness:* Yoga cultivates leadership qualities such as resilience, adaptability, and emotional intelligence, which are essential for professional success. Graduates who practice yoga are equipped with skills that enhance their ability to navigate challenges in the workplace.
- *Research and Innovation:* Universities conduct research on the benefits of yoga in academic and professional settings, contributing to evidence-based practices in education and healthcare. This research informs the development of effective yoga programs tailored to the needs of students and faculty.

Overall Benefits

- *Promotion of Mindfulness:* Yoga teaches students to live mindfully, focusing on the present moment and cultivating self-awareness. Mindfulness practices enhance academic focus, decision-making skills, and interpersonal relationships.
- *Holistic Development:* Integrating yoga into education nurtures holistic development by addressing physical, mental, emotional, and social aspects of student well-being. This approach supports students in becoming well-rounded individuals capable of thriving in diverse environments.
- *Lifelong Wellness Habits:* By practicing yoga in educational settings, students develop lifelong habits of wellness and self-care. These habits contribute to sustained health and happiness throughout their lives, benefiting both individuals and society as a whole.

The importance of integrating yoga in the education sector cannot be overstated. From schools to universities, yoga enhances physical health, promotes emotional resilience, improves academic performance, and fosters a supportive community environment. By integrating yoga into educational curricula and wellness programmes, institutions contribute to the comprehensive development and success of students in today's dynamic world.

Creating a ragging-free environment in educational institutions is a critical goal for ensuring student safety, well-being, and academic success. Ragging, often synonymous with bullying or hazing, can have detrimental effects on students' mental health, confidence, and overall educational experience. Implementing yoga practices can contribute significantly to fostering a positive and respectful campus culture, thereby reducing incidents of ragging. Here's how yoga can help in preparing a ragging-free environment:

Promoting Mindfulness and Self-awareness

- *Mindfulness Practices:* Yoga emphasises mindfulness techniques such as deep breathing, meditation, and body awareness. These practices help students develop self-awareness, emotional regulation, and empathy towards others. By cultivating mindfulness, students become more attuned to their actions and the impact they have on their peers, fostering a culture of respect and sensitivity.
- *Anxiety Reduction:* Yoga is renowned for its ability to reduce stress and anxiety levels. High-stress environments can exacerbate negative behaviours like ragging. Regular practice of yoga techniques, such as *pranayama* (breath control) and gentle *asanas* (postures), helps students manage stress effectively, promoting a calm and supportive atmosphere on campus.

Building Community and Positive Relationships

- *Yoga Clubs and Workshops:* Establishing yoga clubs or offering yoga workshops provides opportunities for students to bond over shared interests in health and wellness. These initiatives create a sense of community and belonging, encouraging positive interactions and mutual respect among peers.
- *Team-building Activities:* Yoga sessions can include partner exercises or group activities that promote collaboration, trust-building, and camaraderie. By participating in these activities, students develop teamwork skills and strengthen interpersonal relationships, reducing the likelihood of divisive behaviours like ragging.

Cultivating Values and Ethical Behavior

- *Yoga Philosophy:* The philosophical teachings of yoga, including principles of non-violence (*ahimsa*), truthfulness (*satya*), and compassion (*karuna*), promote ethical behaviour and respect for others. Integrating these values into campus life through yoga classes or discussions encourages students to uphold these principles in their interactions, thereby creating a harmonious and inclusive environment.

- *Leadership Development:* Yoga practice fosters qualities such as leadership, self-discipline, and self-confidence. Students who embody these qualities are more likely to take on leadership roles in preventing ragging and promoting positive peer relationships within their academic community.

Enhancing Mental Health and Well-being

- *Emotional Resilience:* Yoga enhances emotional resilience by teaching students how to cope with challenges and setbacks effectively. Resilient individuals are less likely to engage in negative behaviours like ragging and more inclined towards supporting and uplifting their peers.
- *Promoting a Healthy Lifestyle:* Beyond physical exercise, yoga encourages a holistic approach to health that includes proper nutrition, adequate sleep, and balanced living. Students who prioritise their well-being are less susceptible to stress-related behaviours that contribute to ragging incidents.

Implementing Policies and Awareness Campaigns

- Policy Enforcement*:* Educational institutions should have strict policies against ragging, clearly outlining consequences for perpetrators. Incorporating yoga into anti-ragging initiatives reinforces the institution's commitment to promoting a safe and respectful environment for all students.
- *Awareness and Education:* Conducting workshops or seminars on the detrimental effects of ragging and the benefits of mindfulness practices like yoga raises awareness among students and faculty. These initiatives encourage dialogue, empathy, and collective responsibility in preventing ragging.

Yoga plays a crucial role in preparing a ragging-free environment in educational institutions by promoting mindfulness, building community, cultivating ethical values, enhancing mental health, and fostering a supportive campus culture. By integrating yoga into educational curricula and campus life, institutions empower students to embrace positive behaviours, respect diversity, and uphold mutual respect, thereby creating a safe and inclusive environment conducive to learning and personal growth.

4

Yoga in Health Sector

Hospitals, Gym, Wellness Centers etc.

In recent years, the practice of yoga has transcended its traditional roots to become an integral component of health circles worldwide, spanning hospitals, gyms, wellness centres, and beyond. This evolution reflects a growing recognition of yoga's profound benefits for physical, mental, and emotional well-being. From alleviating chronic conditions to promoting holistic health, yoga's relevance in diverse health settings is increasingly valued. Here's an exploration of the key benefits:

- *Improved Flexibility and Strength:* Yoga incorporates a variety of *asanas* (postures) that stretch and strengthen muscles, joints, and ligaments. Regular practice enhances flexibility, mobility, and overall physical endurance, which is beneficial for individuals recovering from injuries or managing chronic conditions.
- *Enhanced Cardiovascular Health:* Certain yoga practices, such as dynamic sequences and *pranayama* (breathing exercises), improve circulation, lower blood pressure, and promote heart health. These benefits complement traditional cardiovascular exercise routines.
- *Pain Management:* Yoga has been shown to alleviate pain associated with conditions like arthritis, lower back pain, and migraines. Gentle stretches, relaxation techniques, and mindfulness practices reduce muscle tension and improve pain tolerance.
- *Support for Rehabilitation:* In rehabilitation settings, yoga aids in recovering strength, coordination, and balance following surgery, injury, or illness. Its gentle yet effective approach supports gradual recovery and reduces the risk of re-injury.
- *Relaxation:* Yoga promotes relaxation through deep breathing and meditation practices, which activate the parasympathetic nervous system. This helps reduce stress hormones like cortisol, fostering a sense of calm and emotional balance.
- *Mood Enhancement:* Regular yoga practice boosts serotonin levels and promotes the release of endorphins, neurotransmitters that

elevate mood and reduce symptoms of anxiety and depression. It provides a natural, holistic approach to mental health care.
- *Improved Sleep Quality:* Yoga encourages relaxation and relieves tension, making it easier for individuals to fall asleep and experience deeper, more restorative rest. Better sleep contributes to overall mental clarity and emotional resilience.

Holistic Health Promotion

- *Mind-Body Connection:* Yoga emphasises the connection between the mind and body, promoting awareness of physical sensations, thoughts, and emotions. This holistic approach supports individuals in making informed choices about their health and lifestyle.
- *Enhanced Energy and Vitality:* Through practices like *pranayama* and dynamic *asanas*, yoga increases energy levels and vitality. Participants often report feeling more invigorated, focused, and capable of managing daily challenges effectively.
- *Weight Management:* Yoga complements weight management efforts by improving metabolism, supporting digestion, and promoting mindful eating habits. It encourages a balanced approach to fitness that encompasses both physical activity and mental well-being.

Integration into Health Circles

- *Hospitals and Rehabilitation Centers:* Yoga programmes in hospitals aid in recovery, reduce stress for patients and caregivers, and enhance overall well-being during treatment. Integrative medicine approaches include yoga as part of comprehensive patient care plans.
- *Wellness Centres and Gyms:* Wellness centres and gyms offer yoga classes tailored to various fitness levels and health goals. These classes provide members with opportunities to improve flexibility, strength, and mental clarity in a supportive environment.
- *Corporate Wellness Programmes:* Many workplaces incorporate yoga into corporate wellness initiatives to reduce employee stress, improve productivity, and promote a healthy work-life balance. Yoga sessions during breaks or after work hours contribute to a positive organisational culture.

The relevance of practicing yoga in health circles like hospitals, gyms, and wellness centres lies in its ability to promote holistic health and well-being. From physical fitness and pain management to stress reduction and emotional balance, yoga offers a versatile approach to enhancing quality of life for individuals of all ages and backgrounds. As its benefits continue to be supported by scientific research and embraced by health professionals, yoga's role in modern healthcare is poised to expand, enriching lives and empowering individuals on their journey towards optimal health.

Approach of Modern Health System

Modern health systems approach disease management through a structured and multidisciplinary framework aimed at diagnosing, treating, and preventing illnesses to improve patient outcomes and overall public health. Here's an overview of the key strategies and components involved in tackling diseases within the modern health system:

Diagnosis and Assessment

- *Medical Evaluation:* Diseases are identified through comprehensive medical evaluations that include patient history, physical examinations, and diagnostic tests such as imaging (X-rays, MRIs) and laboratory tests (blood tests, biopsies).
- *Advanced Technology:* Modern health systems utilize advanced technologies and medical equipment for accurate diagnosis. This includes genetic testing, molecular diagnostics, and digital health tools that facilitate remote monitoring and real-time data analysis.
- *Multidisciplinary Approach*: Specialists from various medical disciplines collaborate to analyse complex cases and determine the most effective diagnostic approach. This may involve consultations between primary care physicians, specialists, surgeons, radiologists, and pathologists.

Treatment Modalities

- *Evidence-based Medicine:* Treatment decisions are guided by evidence-based practices derived from clinical trials, research studies, and medical guidelines. These practices ensure that treatments are effective, safe, and tailored to individual patient needs.
- *Pharmaceutical Interventions:* Medications, including antibiotics, chemotherapy drugs, and biologics, are prescribed to manage symptoms, control disease progression, or eradicate infections.

Pharmacogenomics may be employed to personalise drug therapies based on genetic factors.

- *Surgical Interventions:* Surgeons perform procedures ranging from minimally invasive surgeries to complex organ transplants to treat diseases that require direct intervention or correction.
- *Interventional Therapies:* Procedures such as angioplasty, radiation therapy, and stem cell transplants are utilised to target specific disease processes or conditions, often in collaboration with medical and radiation oncologists.

Disease Management and Prevention

- *Chronic Disease Management:* Health systems implement chronic disease management programs to monitor and support patients with conditions like diabetes, hypertension, and cardiovascular diseases. These programmes emphasise lifestyle modifications, adherence to medications, and regular follow-up care.
- *Preventive Care:* Preventive measures, including vaccinations, screenings (e.g., mammograms, colonoscopies), and health education initiatives, aim to detect diseases early or prevent them altogether. Public health campaigns promote healthy behaviours and reduce risk factors such as smoking, poor diet, and sedentary lifestyles.
- *Health Promotion:* Health systems prioritise wellness and disease prevention through community outreach programs, health fairs, and partnerships with local organisations. These initiatives raise awareness, provide resources, and empower individuals to make informed health decisions.

Integration of Technology and Innovation

- *Telemedicine and Digital Health:* Telehealth platforms enable remote consultations, virtual visits, and telemonitoring of patients, expanding access to healthcare services and improving patient engagement.
- *Artificial Intelligence (AI):* AI-driven algorithms analyse medical data, predict disease trends, and assist in clinical decision-making. Machine learning models enhance diagnostics, identify treatment patterns, and optimise healthcare delivery.
- *Precision Medicine:* Tailored therapies based on genetic, environmental, and lifestyle factors enable personalised treatment plans that improve outcomes and minimise adverse effects.

Quality Improvement and Patient Safety

- *Clinical Pathways and Protocols:* Standardised protocols and clinical pathways streamline care delivery, enhance patient safety, and optimise resource utilisation within healthcare facilities.
- *Patient-centred Care:* Health systems prioritise patient preferences, values, and cultural beliefs in treatment planning and care delivery, fostering trust and collaboration between healthcare providers and patients.

The modern health system's approach to tackling diseases combines scientific advancements, multidisciplinary collaboration, patient-centred care, and preventive strategies to achieve optimal health outcomes. By integrating cutting-edge technology, evidence-based practices, and comprehensive disease management protocols, health systems strive to address current health challenges while preparing for future healthcare needs. Continuous innovation, research, and public health initiatives are key to advancing disease prevention, treatment, and ultimately improving the overall health and well-being of populations worldwide.

Comparison between Modern Medical Treatments and Natural Healing Techniques

In the realm of healthcare, the comparison between modern medical treatments and natural healing techniques like yoga often highlights stark differences in approaches, outcomes, and considerations of side effects. While modern health systems rely heavily on pharmaceutical interventions and invasive procedures to manage diseases and symptoms, yoga offers a holistic alternative rooted in ancient wisdom and mindfulness practices.

Modern Health System: Pharmaceutical and Invasive Treatments

Modern medicine excels in diagnosing complex diseases and providing immediate interventions through pharmaceutical drugs, surgeries, and other invasive procedures. Here are key aspects of the modern health system:

- *Pharmaceutical Interventions:* Medications play a crucial role in treating acute conditions and chronic diseases. From antibiotics to chemotherapy drugs, pharmaceuticals target specific biochemical pathways to alleviate symptoms or eradicate pathogens.

- *Surgical Procedures:* Surgeons perform intricate procedures to correct anatomical abnormalities, remove tumors, replace joints, and perform organ transplants. These interventions are essential for life-saving treatments and restoring bodily functions.
- *Advanced Medical Technology:* Modern health systems leverage cutting-edge technologies such as imaging scans (MRI, CT), robotic surgeries, and genetic testing. These innovations enhance diagnostic accuracy and treatment precision.
- *Evidence-based Medicine:* Treatment decisions are guided by rigorous clinical trials, research studies, and medical guidelines. Healthcare providers adhere to standardised protocols to ensure patient safety and optimise therapeutic outcomes.

Challenges and Side Effects of Modern Medicine

- *Side Effects:* Many pharmaceutical drugs carry potential side effects ranging from mild discomfort to severe complications. Patients may experience adverse reactions, allergies, or long-term health consequences, necessitating careful monitoring and management.
- *Dependency on Medications:* Chronic use of medications can lead to dependency, drug interactions, and the development of drug-resistant strains of pathogens. Managing polypharmacy (multiple medications) poses challenges in balancing therapeutic benefits with potential risks.
- *Invasive Procedures:* Surgeries and invasive treatments carry inherent risks such as infections, anesthesia complications, and post-operative recovery challenges. Patients may require prolonged hospital stays and rehabilitation periods.

Yoga as a Natural Healing Technique

Yoga, originating from ancient Indian philosophy, offers a holistic approach to health and well-being that emphasises harmony between the mind, body, and spirit. Here's how yoga contrasts with modern medical practices:

- *Mindfulness and Stress Reduction:* Yoga integrates mindfulness practices, including *pranayama* (breathing techniques) and meditation, to reduce stress, promote relaxation, and enhance mental clarity. These techniques strengthen the mind-body connection and support overall emotional well-being.

- *Physical Benefits:* Yoga *asanas* (postures) improve flexibility, strength, and balance without the physical strain associated with high-impact exercises or surgeries. Gentle movements and stretches alleviate muscle tension, improve circulation, and support joint health.
- *Non-invasive and Low Risk:* Unlike surgical procedures and pharmaceutical drugs, yoga poses minimal risk of adverse effects. Practitioners can adapt practices to individual needs and health conditions, making it accessible for diverse populations, including older adults and individuals with chronic illnesses.
- *Complementary Therapy:* Yoga serves as a complementary therapy in integrative medicine, supporting conventional treatments by reducing pain, enhancing immune function, and improving quality of life for patients undergoing cancer treatment, chronic pain management, or mental health care.

Evidence-based Benefits of Yoga

Research Support: Scientific studies validate the therapeutic benefits of yoga in managing chronic conditions such as hypertension, diabetes, depression, and anxiety. Evidence suggests yoga reduces inflammation markers, improves cardiovascular health, and enhances cognitive function.

Long-term Health Promotion: Regular practice of yoga cultivates healthy lifestyle habits, including mindful eating, adequate sleep, and stress management. These habits contribute to long-term wellness, disease prevention, and overall quality of life.

Choosing the Right Approach

The comparison between modern health systems and yoga highlights the significance of personalised healthcare choices based on individual needs, preferences, and health conditions. While modern medicine excels in acute care and surgical interventions, yoga offers a natural, holistic approach to health maintenance and disease prevention with minimal side effects. Integrating both approaches through collaborative care models allows patients to benefit from comprehensive, patient-centred treatments that optimise health outcomes and enhance overall well-being. Ultimately, informed decision-making and a balanced approach to healthcare empower individuals to achieve optimal health through the best-suited interventions for their unique circumstances.

The comparison between modern health systems and yoga highlights contrasting yet complementary approaches to healthcare, each offering distinct benefits tailored to individual health needs and preferences. Modern medicine, with its emphasis on technological advancements, pharmaceutical interventions, and surgical procedures, excels in acute care settings and complex medical conditions requiring immediate attention. Here's how modern health systems and yoga differ and converge in promoting health and well-being:

Modern Health Systems: Focus on Acute Care and Interventions

Modern healthcare relies on sophisticated diagnostic tools, such as MRI and CT scans, to accurately diagnose and treat diseases. These technologies enable healthcare providers to identify conditions at early stages and intervene promptly. Medications play a pivotal role in managing symptoms, controlling chronic diseases, and combating infections. Pharmaceutical advancements continue to develop targeted therapies that address specific molecular pathways, enhancing treatment efficacy. Surgeons perform intricate procedures to treat conditions ranging from appendicitis to complex cardiac surgeries and organ transplants. Surgical interventions are crucial for correcting anatomical defects, removing tumors, and restoring bodily functions. Hospitals and emergency departments provide essential care for life-threatening conditions, trauma, and acute medical emergencies. Prompt medical intervention and intensive care support are critical in saving lives and stabilising patients.

Yoga: Holistic Approach to Health Maintenance and Prevention

Yoga emphasises the integration of physical postures (*asanas*), breathing techniques (*pranayama*), and meditation to promote mental clarity, emotional balance, and physical well-being. These practices enhance the mind-body connection, fostering overall health. Mindfulness techniques taught in yoga classes, such as deep breathing and guided meditation, help reduce stress hormones like cortisol. Regular practice promotes relaxation, improves sleep quality, and boosts resilience to daily stressors. Yoga *asanas* improve flexibility, strength, and balance through gentle stretching and muscle engagement. These physical benefits support joint health, alleviate chronic pain, and enhance overall mobility without the risks associated with high-impact exercises. Yoga serves as a complementary therapy alongside conventional medical treatments. It supports recovery from surgeries, manages chronic conditions like hypertension and diabetes, and aids in mental health care by reducing symptoms of anxiety and depression.

Integration for Optimal Health Outcomes

Integrating modern healthcare and yoga through collaborative care models allows for personalised treatment plans that address holistic health needs. Healthcare providers collaborate to combine evidence-based medical interventions with holistic approaches to optimise patient outcomes. Empowering patients to make informed decisions about their health involves considering individual preferences, values, and lifestyle choices. Integrating yoga into treatment plans encourages patients to actively participate in their own care, promoting a sense of empowerment and well-being. While modern medicine focuses on treating existing conditions, yoga emphasises preventive health measures through lifestyle modifications and stress management. This proactive approach reduces the incidence of chronic diseases and improves overall quality of life.

The comparison between modern health systems and yoga highlights the importance of personalised healthcare choices that prioritise individual needs, preferences, and health conditions. While modern medicine excels in acute care and surgical interventions, yoga offers a natural, holistic approach to health maintenance and disease prevention with minimal side effects. Integrating both approaches through collaborative care models empowers patients to achieve optimal health outcomes and enhance overall well-being. By embracing a balanced approach to healthcare that combines advanced medical treatments with holistic practices like yoga, individuals can navigate their health journeys with confidence and resilience, ensuring comprehensive care that addresses their unique circumstances and promotes lifelong wellness.

5

Yoga and Entrepreneurship

Yoga, traditionally known for its physical, mental, and spiritual benefits, has also emerged as a fertile ground for entrepreneurial opportunities. The increasing global popularity of yoga has created a demand for a wide range of products and services, enabling individuals to leverage their passion for yoga into successful business ventures. Here's how yoga can provide avenues for entrepreneurship:

Yoga Instruction and Studios

- *Yoga Studios:* Opening a yoga studio is one of the most direct ways to transform a passion for yoga into a business. Studios offer classes across various yoga styles (e.g., *Hatha, Vinyasa, Ashtanga*), catering to different skill levels and preferences.
- *Private Instruction:* Offering one-on-one yoga sessions or small group classes can be a lucrative business. Personalised instruction often commands a premium, as it caters to individuals seeking customised yoga experiences.
- *Online Classes:* The rise of digital platforms has enabled yoga instructors to reach a global audience. Virtual classes, pre-recorded sessions, and live-streamed workshops can be offered through platforms like YouTube, Zoom, or specialised yoga apps.

Yoga-Related Products

- *Yoga Apparel and Accessories:* Designing and selling yoga-specific clothing (e.g., leggings, tops, and sports bras) and accessories (e.g., mats, blocks, straps) is a thriving market. Entrepreneurs can create brands that emphasise sustainability, style, and functionality.
- *Health and Wellness Products:* Expanding into health and wellness products, such as essential oils, herbal teas, and supplements that complement yoga practice, can attract health-conscious consumers.

Wellness Retreats and Workshops

- *Yoga Retreats:* Organising yoga retreats in tranquil locations can provide immersive experiences for practitioners. These retreats often combine yoga with other wellness activities like meditation, detox programmes, and nature excursions.
- *Workshops and Trainings:* Hosting specialised workshops, teacher training programmes, and certification courses can attract both novice practitioners and aspiring yoga instructors. These events can be conducted in-person or online.

Corporate Wellness Programmes

Corporate Yoga: Offering yoga classes and wellness programmes to corporations can address employee well-being, reduce stress, and enhance productivity. Corporate wellness has become a significant focus for many businesses, providing a lucrative market for yoga entrepreneurs.

Yoga Therapy

Therapeutic Yoga: Developing a practice focused on yoga therapy to address specific health conditions (e.g., chronic pain, anxiety, depression) can be both impactful and profitable. This niche requires additional training and certification but meets a growing demand for holistic health solutions.

Content Creation and Education

Books and Publications: Writing books, creating e-books, or publishing guides on yoga practice, philosophy, and lifestyle can reach a broad audience. This includes how-to guides, personal memoirs, and research-based publications.

Online Platforms and Apps: Developing websites, blogs, or apps that offer yoga-related content, from instructional videos to articles on wellness, can generate revenue through subscriptions, advertisements, and affiliate marketing.

Collaborations and Partnerships

In today's interconnected world, the potential for collaborations and partnerships within the yoga community and beyond has significantly expanded. These collaborations offer unique opportunities to enhance the practice and impact of yoga, broaden its accessibility, and integrate it with various fields to promote overall well-being. Here's an in-depth look at yoga collaborations and partnerships, their benefits, and examples of successful initiatives.

Benefits of Yoga Collaborations and Partnerships

- *Increased Accessibility:* Reaching Diverse Populations: Partnerships with community centers, schools, and healthcare facilities can bring yoga to diverse populations, including those who might not otherwise have access.

  Financial Support: Collaborations with sponsors and donors can provide financial support, making yoga classes more affordable or even free for underprivileged communities.
- *Enhanced Learning and Innovation:* Cross-disciplinary Integration: Collaborations with professionals from different fields (e.g., healthcare, education, sports) can lead to innovative approaches and techniques in yoga practice and teaching.

  Resource Sharing: Partnerships enable the sharing of resources, knowledge, and expertise, enriching the yoga experience for practitioners.
- *Broadened Impact:* Holistic Wellness Programs: Integrating yoga with other wellness practices (e.g., nutrition, mental health services) through partnerships can create comprehensive wellness programmes.

  Corporate Wellness: Collaborating with businesses to offer corporate wellness programmes can enhance employee well-being, productivity, and job satisfaction.
- *Community Building:* Social Connections: Collaborations foster a sense of community and connection among practitioners, creating supportive networks.

  Cultural Exchange: International partnerships can promote cultural exchange and understanding, broadening the horizons of yoga practitioners.

Examples of Yoga Collaborations and Partnerships

- *Yoga and Healthcare:* Hospitals and Clinics: Integrating yoga into healthcare settings for rehabilitation, chronic disease management, and mental health support.

  Yoga Therapy Programmes: Collaborating with therapists and counselors to offer yoga therapy for individuals dealing with trauma, anxiety, and depression.

- *Yoga and Education:* Schools and Universities: Implementing yoga programmes in schools and universities to promote physical health, mental clarity, and stress management among students.

  Teacher Training Programs: Partnering with educational institutions to develop comprehensive yoga teacher training programmes.
- *Yoga and Corporations:* Corporate Wellness Initiatives: Partnering with businesses to provide yoga classes, workshops, and retreats for employees, enhancing workplace wellness.

  Team-building Activities: Using yoga and mindfulness exercises as part of corporate team-building activities to improve collaboration and communication.
- *Yoga and Non-profits:* Community Outreach Programs: Collaborating with non-profits to offer yoga in underserved communities, shelters, and rehabilitation centers.

  Special Events and Fundraisers: Partnering for special events like charity yoga classes or wellness festivals to raise awareness and funds for various causes.
- *Yoga and Technology:* Online Platforms: Partnering with tech companies to develop and deliver online yoga classes and virtual workshops, making yoga accessible to a global audience.

  Health Apps: Integrating yoga practices into health and wellness apps to provide guided sessions, tracking, and personalised recommendations.

Successful Examples of Yoga Collaborations

- *Veterans' Yoga Project:* Partnership with VA Hospitals: This project collaborates with Veterans Affairs hospitals to provide yoga and mindfulness practices tailored for veterans dealing with PTSD and other service-related issues.

  Veterans Yoga Project is a national 501(c)3 organisation on a mission to support recovery and resilience among our veterans, military families, and communities. VYP envisions a future where all those affected by trauma have access to a full range of mind-body practices and programmes, and is committed to providing these tools and training in Safer, Predictable, and Controlled environments (SPaCe).

  Founded in 2011, Veterans Yoga Project is an IAYT member school, an NBCC Approved Continuing Education Provider, and a certified Yoga Alliance School (RYS-200, YACEP). Working in partnership with veterans, active-duty military personnel, student veterans' organisations, veterans' treatment courts, and other non-profit organisations, VYP-trained instructors and clinicians provide programmes, resources, connections, and teach over 100 free yoga classes each week.

- *Yoga in Schools Initiative:* Collaboration with Educational Institutions: Various programmes partner with schools to incorporate yoga into the curriculum, aiming to improve students' physical health, emotional regulation, and academic performance.
- *Corporate Yoga Programmes:* Partnership with Major Corporations: Companies like Google and Apple have integrated yoga and mindfulness programs into their corporate wellness initiatives, providing regular classes and wellness retreats for employees.
- *Non-profit Yoga Outreach:* Yoga Foster: This non-profit collaborates with schools to train teachers and provide resources to bring yoga into classrooms, focusing on underserved communities.

Yoga collaborations and partnerships have the potential to significantly enhance the reach, impact, and effectiveness of yoga practices. By working together with various sectors such as healthcare, education, corporate, non-profits, and technology, the yoga community can create synergies that promote holistic well-being, foster innovation, and build stronger, more connected communities. Embracing these partnerships allows for a more inclusive and expansive approach to yoga, ensuring that its benefits can be shared widely and effectively.

Brand Partnerships: Collaborating with existing brands to promote yoga-related products or services can be mutually beneficial. Influencers and experienced practitioners often partner with brands for marketing campaigns, leveraging their following and expertise.

Wellness Centers: Partnering with wellness centers, spas, and gyms to offer yoga classes and workshops can expand an entrepreneur's reach and provide additional revenue streams.

Keys to Success in Yoga Entrepreneurship

- *Authenticity and Expertise:* Establishing credibility and trust is crucial. This requires genuine expertise, continual learning, and a commitment to the core principles of yoga.

- *Market Understanding:* Identifying and understanding the target market is essential. Tailoring services and products to meet the specific needs and preferences of different demographics can enhance business success.
- *Innovation and Adaptability:* Staying innovative and adaptable in response to trends, technological advancements, and customer feedback ensures the business remains relevant and competitive.
- *Community Building:* Fostering a sense of community among clients and followers helps build loyalty and word-of-mouth referrals. Engaging with the community through social media, events, and regular communication is key.

Yoga offers a pletora of entrepreneurial opportunities across different domains, from instruction and product sales to retreats and digital content creation. By leveraging their passion and expertise, yoga entrepreneurs can establish successful businesses that not only generate income but also promote health, wellness, and holistic living. Embracing authenticity, understanding market needs, and fostering a strong community connection are essential elements for thriving in the yoga entrepreneurship landscape.

The relationship between yoga and entrepreneurship is symbiotic. Yoga enhances the personal qualities necessary for successful entrepreneurship while providing ample business opportunities in the wellness sector. Entrepreneurs who practice yoga benefit from improved mental clarity, stress management, physical health, and emotional intelligence, all of which contribute to their effectiveness and resilience. Meanwhile, the growing popularity of yoga creates diverse opportunities for entrepreneurial ventures, from teaching and training to product development and digital innovation. Embracing both the practice of yoga and its entrepreneurial possibilities can lead to a fulfilling, balanced, and prosperous career.

Problems of Society and Solutions through Practicing Yoga in Daily Life

Society today faces a myriad of challenges, ranging from mental health crises and physical health issues to social disconnection and environmental stress. As these problems proliferate, individuals seek holistic and sustainable solutions to enhance their well-being and foster a more harmonious existence. Practicing yoga in daily life offers profound benefits that address these societal challenges by promoting physical health, mental clarity, emotional balance, and social cohesion. Here's a detailed exploration of the problems facing society and how yoga can provide effective solutions.

Mental Health Issues

Mental health disorders, including anxiety, depression, and stress-related conditions, are increasingly prevalent. Factors such as work pressures, social media, and fast-paced lifestyles contribute to mental strain and emotional distress.

- *Stress Reduction:* Yoga practices, such as *pranayama* (breath control) and meditation, activate the parasympathetic nervous system, reducing stress hormones like cortisol. Regular practice helps individuals manage stress more effectively.
- *Improved Mental Clarity*: *Asanas* (yoga postures) and mindfulness practices enhance mental focus and clarity, reducing symptoms of anxiety and depression.
- *Emotional Balance:* Yoga fosters emotional regulation, helping practitioners maintain a positive outlook and cope better with life's challenges.

Physical Health Problems

Chronic diseases such as obesity, hypertension, diabetes, and cardiovascular issues are on the rise due to sedentary lifestyles and poor dietary habits.

- *Enhanced Physical Fitness:* Regular yoga practice improves flexibility, strength, and cardiovascular health, aiding in weight management and overall physical fitness.
- *Chronic Disease Management:* Yoga can complement medical treatments by improving circulation, lowering blood pressure, and enhancing respiratory function, thus helping manage chronic conditions.
- *Pain Relief:* Specific yoga postures alleviate musculoskeletal pain, particularly in the back, neck, and joints, providing a non-invasive way to manage chronic pain.

Social Disconnection

Modern society often fosters social isolation and disconnection, exacerbated by urbanisation, technology, and individualistic lifestyles. This social disconnection can lead to loneliness and a lack of community support.

- Community Building: Yoga classes and workshops create a sense of community, encouraging social interaction and support networks. Practitioners often form lasting bonds, fostering a sense of belonging.
- *Enhanced Empathy:* Yoga emphasizes compassion and mindfulness, improving interpersonal relationships and promoting a sense of empathy and understanding among individuals.
- *Inclusive Practice:* Yoga is accessible to people of all ages, backgrounds, and physical abilities, making it an inclusive activity that bridges social gaps and fosters unity.

Environmental Stress

Environmental issues such as pollution, climate change, and urban noise contribute to stress and anxiety. The fast-paced, technology-driven lifestyle further disconnects people from nature.

- *Mindfulness and Nature Connection:* Yoga encourages mindfulness and a deeper connection with the environment. Practices such as outdoor yoga sessions can enhance appreciation for nature and promote eco-conscious living.
- *Sustainable Lifestyle:* The principles of yoga advocate for simplicity and sustainability, encouraging practices that reduce environmental impact, such as mindful consumption and minimalism.
- *Stress Relief:* By reducing overall stress levels, yoga helps individuals cope better with environmental stressors, fostering a sense of inner peace and resilience.

Ethical and Moral Challenges

Ethical dilemmas and moral conflicts arise from societal issues such as inequality, corruption, and lack of integrity. These challenges erode trust and harmony within communities.

- *Ethical Living:* Yoga's foundational principles, such as yamas (ethical guidelines) and niyamas (personal observances), promote ethical behaviour, including non-violence, truthfulness, and contentment.
- *Increased Awareness:* Yoga fosters self-awareness and reflection, helping individuals align their actions with their values and principles.

- *Social Responsibility:* Practicing yoga encourages a sense of responsibility towards others and the community, promoting altruistic behaviour and social justice.

Practicing yoga in daily life offers a holistic approach to addressing many of society's pressing problems. By fostering mental clarity, physical health, emotional balance, and social cohesion, yoga provides sustainable solutions that enhance individual well-being and promote a harmonious society. The integration of yoga principles into everyday life encourages mindful living, ethical behaviour, and a deeper connection with the environment and community, paving the way for a healthier, more balanced, and connected world. Through regular practice and commitment to its teachings, yoga can transform lives and contribute significantly to resolving the challenges facing modern society.

6

Yoga for Children and Adolescence

Adolescence is a phase of life where individuals are at a turning point in emotional and physical development. They need to become industrious and engaged in planning and executing tasks. They have different interests, abilities, and personalities. To understand this phase let's start with a story: In a small town nestled among rolling hills and whispering trees, lived a young girl named Mia. At twelve years old, Mia was like any other child, full of dreams and energy, but she faced her own set of challenges. Mia struggled with anxiety and often felt overwhelmed by schoolwork and the social dynamics of her peers. Her parents, concerned for her well-being, sought ways to help her find balance and peace.

One sunny afternoon, Mia's mother, Sarah, came across a flyer for a local yoga studio that offered classes specifically for children and adolescents. Intrigued by the potential benefits, Sarah decided to enroll Mia in the Saturday morning class. Little did they know, this decision would set Mia on a path of transformation.

First Steps into Yoga

On the first day of class, Mia walked into the yoga studio with a mix of curiosity and apprehension. The studio was a warm, inviting space filled with soft lighting, colorful mats, and a gentle scent of lavender. The instructor, Miss Lily, greeted each child with a warm smile and a calming presence. She explained that yoga was not just about physical postures, but also about finding inner peace and strength.

Miss Lily began the class with simple breathing exercises, encouraging the children to close their eyes and focus on their breath. Mia felt a sense of calm wash over her as she followed along. The session progressed to basic yoga poses, each one designed to improve flexibility, strength, and balance. Miss Lily's instructions were clear and encouraging, making everyone feel at ease.

Discovering Inner Strength

As weeks turned into months, Mia began to notice subtle changes within herself. The breathing exercises she learned in class became her secret weapon against anxiety. Whenever she felt nervous before a test or overwhelmed by homework, she would take a few deep breaths, grounding herself in the present moment. The physical postures, once challenging, now felt like a natural extension of her body. She moved with more confidence and grace, both on and off the mat.

One day, Miss Lily introduced the concept of mindfulness. She taught the children how to pay attention to their thoughts and emotions without judgment. For Mia, this was a revelation. She realised that her worries and fears did not define her; they were just passing clouds in the sky of her mind. This newfound awareness allowed her to navigate her emotions with greater ease and resilience.

Building Resilience and Community

Yoga also fostered a sense of community among the children in the class. Mia made new friends who shared her journey of self-discovery. They supported each other, celebrating small victories and offering encouragement during challenging poses. This sense of belonging extended beyond the studio, positively impacting Mia's social interactions at school.

One memorable Saturday, Miss Lily organized a yoga retreat for the children. They spent the day in nature, practicing yoga under the open sky, meditating by a serene lake, and sharing their thoughts and experiences around a campfire. The retreat reinforced the lessons they had learned in the studio and deepened their connection with nature and each other.

The Ripple Effect

The benefits of yoga rippled through Mia's life in unexpected ways. Her improved focus and concentration helped her excel in her studies. She became more compassionate and patient, not just with herself but with others. Her parents noticed that she smiled more often and seemed genuinely happier.

Mia's story inspired other families in the community to explore yoga. Soon, the studio offered more classes for children and adolescents, each one filled with eager participants. Parents, teachers, and even school counselors began to recognise the profound impact yoga had on the children's well-being.

A Lifelong Practice

As Mia grew older, yoga remained a cornerstone of her life. It was not just a practice but a way of living. The lessons she learned on the mat – resilience, mindfulness, compassion – guided her through the ups and downs of adolescence and beyond. She often shared her journey with others, encouraging them to find their path to inner peace and strength.

The story of Mia illustrates the transformative power of yoga for children and adolescents. In a world where young people face numerous pressures and challenges, yoga offers a sanctuary of calm and a toolkit for navigating life's complexities. It fosters physical health, emotional resilience, and a sense of community, laying the foundation for a balanced and fulfilling life. As more families and communities embrace yoga, its benefits will continue to ripple outward, creating a generation of mindful, compassionate, and empowered individuals.

Significance of Yoga Practice for Adolescence

Adolescence is a critical period of development characterised by significant physical, emotional, and psychological changes. It is a time of self-discovery, identity formation, and increased social pressures. Amidst these challenges, the practice of yoga offers numerous benefits that can support adolescents through this transformative phase. Here's a detailed exploration of the significance of yoga practice for adolescents:

Physical Benefits

- *Improved Flexibility and Strength:*
  - *Flexibility:* Yoga involves a range of poses that stretch and elongate muscles, improving flexibility. This can help adolescents avoid injuries in daily activities and sports.
  - *Strength:* Many yoga poses require the use of body weight for resistance, which helps in building muscular strength. Strong muscles support proper posture and overall physical stability.
- *Enhanced Balance and Coordination:*
  - Balance: Yoga poses that challenge balance help develop proprioception, the sense of body position in space. Improved balance is beneficial for physical activities and sports.
  - Coordination: Practicing sequences of movements in yoga enhances coordination, helping adolescents perform daily tasks and physical activities more efficiently.

- *Better Posture:*
  - Adolescents often develop poor posture due to prolonged sitting and the use of digital devices. Yoga emphasises alignment and awareness of body positioning, which promotes better posture and reduces the risk of developing musculoskeletal issues.
- *Promotes Healthy Growth*:
  - Yoga supports overall physical development by encouraging healthy movement patterns and promoting bone and muscle health. This is particularly important during the growth spurts of adolescence.

Mental and Emotional Benefits

- *Stress Reduction:*
  - Breathing Techniques: Yoga teaches various *pranayama* (breathing techniques) that help calm the nervous system and reduce stress. These techniques can be particularly useful during exams and stressful situations.
  - Relaxation: Practices such as sav*asana* (corpse pose) and guided relaxation help in releasing tension and promoting a state of calm.
- *Improved Concentration and Focus:*
  - Yoga requires mindfulness and concentration, which can enhance cognitive functions. Adolescents who practice yoga often find improvements in their ability to concentrate on studies and other tasks.
- *Emotional Regulation:*
  - Adolescence is a time of intense emotions and mood swings. Yoga encourages self-awareness and mindfulness, helping adolescents recognise and manage their emotions more effectively. This leads to better emotional regulation and a more balanced state of mind.
- *Enhanced Self-esteem and Confidence:*
  - Successfully learning and mastering yoga poses can boost an adolescent's self-esteem and confidence. The non-competitive nature of yoga fosters a positive self-image and self-acceptance.

Social Benefits

- *Sense of Community:*
  - Participating in yoga classes can create a sense of community and belonging. Adolescents can form supportive relationships with peers who share similar interests and challenges.

- *Improved Social Skills:*
  - Yoga often involves group activities and partner poses, which can enhance communication and teamwork skills. These social interactions help adolescents develop better interpersonal skills.

Cognitive Benefits

- *Better Academic Performance:*
  - The focus and concentration developed through yoga can translate to better academic performance. Yoga practices improve attention span and memory, aiding in learning and retention of information.
- *Creativity and Problem-solving:*
  - Yoga encourages a state of mindfulness and mental clarity, which can enhance creative thinking and problem-solving abilities. Adolescents can approach challenges with a more open and innovative mindset.

Holistic Development

- *Mind-Body Connection:*
  - Yoga fosters a deep connection between the mind and body, promoting holistic health. Adolescents learn to listen to their bodies and understand the interplay between their physical and mental states.
- *Spiritual Growth:*
  - For those interested, yoga can also offer spiritual benefits, promoting a sense of inner peace and connectedness. This can provide a deeper sense of purpose and fulfillment during the often turbulent adolescent years.

The practice of yoga offers a multitude of benefits for adolescents, addressing their physical, mental, emotional, social, and cognitive needs. By integrating yoga into their daily lives, adolescents can navigate the challenges of this developmental stage with greater ease and resilience. Yoga fosters a balanced and healthy lifestyle, promoting overall well-being and setting the foundation for a positive future. As more schools, communities, and families recognise the value of yoga, its practice can become a cornerstone of adolescent development, supporting young individuals in their journey towards adulthood.

Transformative Impact of Yoga on a Child's Life

Yoga, with its ancient roots and holistic approach, offers profound benefits that can significantly impact a child's physical, mental, emotional, and social well-being. Integrating yoga into a child's life can foster positive growth and development, laying a strong foundation for a healthy and balanced adulthood. Yoga offers a comprehensive approach to nurturing a child's development, addressing physical, mental, emotional, and social dimensions. By incorporating yoga into their daily routine, children can build a strong foundation for a healthy, balanced, and resilient life. The practice not only enhances physical health and cognitive abilities but also promotes emotional stability, social skills, and overall well-being. As yoga becomes more integrated into schools, communities, and homes, its transformative power can significantly enrich the lives of children, preparing them for the challenges and opportunities of the future.

7

Yoga for Women

Women face a wide range of challenges throughout their lives, many of which are shaped by cultural, social, economic, and biological factors. These challenges can vary greatly depending on geographic location, socioeconomic status, ethnicity, and individual circumstances.

Key Challenges for Women

Below are some of the key challenges that women may encounter:

Gender Inequality and Discrimination

- *Workplace Discrimination:* Women often face gender bias in hiring, promotions, and pay. They may also encounter glass ceilings that prevent them from advancing to top leadership positions.
- *Educational Inequality:* In some regions, girls have less access to education compared to boys, which can limit their future opportunities.
- *Political Underrepresentation:* Women are often underrepresented in political offices and decision-making roles, affecting their ability to influence policies that impact their lives.

Health and Reproductive Rights

- *Access to Healthcare:* Women may face barriers to accessing quality healthcare, including reproductive health services.
- *Reproductive Rights:* In many places, women's reproductive rights are restricted, limiting their control over their own bodies and reproductive choices.
- *Maternal Health:* Complications during pregnancy and childbirth can pose significant risks to women's health, especially in areas with inadequate healthcare services.

Violence and Safety

- *Domestic Violence:* Many women experience domestic violence and intimate partner violence, which can have severe physical and psychological impacts.

- *Sexual Harassment and Assault:* Women are often at risk of sexual harassment and assault in various settings, including the workplace, educational institutions, and public spaces.
- *Human Trafficking:* Women and girls are disproportionately affected by human trafficking for purposes of sexual exploitation and forced labour.

Economic Challenges

- *Poverty:* Women are more likely than men to live in poverty, especially single mothers and elderly women.
- *Unpaid Labour:* Women often shoulder the majority of unpaid domestic and caregiving work, which can limit their economic opportunities and financial independence.
- *Economic Dependency:* Limited access to financial resources and employment opportunities can lead to economic dependency on male partners or family members.

Social and Cultural Pressures

- *Gender Roles:* Traditional gender roles and expectations can restrict women's opportunities and dictate their behaviour, limiting their personal and professional growth.
- *Body Image and Beauty Standards:* Societal pressures regarding beauty standards can affect women's self-esteem and mental health.
- *Balancing Multiple Roles:* Women often juggle multiple roles as caregivers, professionals, and community members, leading to stress and burnout.

Educational and Career Barriers

- *STEM Fields:* Women are underrepresented in STEM (Science, Technology, Engineering, and Mathematics) fields, facing biases and lack of support.
- *Work-Life Balance:* Balancing career aspirations with family responsibilities can be challenging, particularly in environments that lack supportive policies such as parental leave and flexible work arrangements.

Legal and Policy Issues

- *Legal Protections:* In many places, women lack legal protections against discrimination, violence, and exploitation.

- *Property and Inheritance Rights:* In some cultures, women have limited rights to inherit property or own land, affecting their economic security and independence.

Mental Health Challenges

- *Mental Health Stigma:* Women may face stigma when seeking mental health care, compounded by the pressures of their multiple roles and responsibilities.
- *Psychological Impact of Abuse:* The trauma from various forms of abuse (domestic violence, sexual assault) can lead to long-term mental health issues.

Access to Resources and Opportunities

- *Digital Divide:* Women, especially in developing countries, often have less access to digital technology and the internet, limiting their access to information and opportunities.
- *Networking and Mentorship:* Women may have fewer opportunities for networking and mentorship, which are crucial for career advancement.

Addressing the Challenges

To effectively address the challenges faced by women, a multifaceted approach is needed, including:

- *Policy Changes:* Implementing and enforcing laws that protect women's rights and promote gender equality.
- *Education and Awareness:* Raising awareness about gender issues and providing education that empowers women and girls.
- *Economic Empowerment:* Providing women with access to economic resources, including education, training, and financial services.
- *Healthcare Access:* Ensuring that women have access to comprehensive healthcare services, including reproductive health.
- *Support Systems:* Creating support systems such as counseling, shelters for abuse survivors, and community networks.

By addressing these challenges through concerted efforts at individual, community, and policy levels, society can move towards greater gender equality and improve the overall well-being of women.

Benefits of Practicing Asana and Pranayama in Women's Life

Practicing *Asana* (physical postures) and *Pranayama* (breathing exercises) can offer numerous benefits to women, enhancing their physical, mental, and emotional well-being. Here's a detailed look at the various benefits:

Physical Benefits

- *Improved Flexibility and Strength:*
  - Flexibility: Regular practice of *asanas* helps to stretch and lengthen muscles, increasing flexibility and range of motion.
  - Strength: Many *asanas* require the use of body weight for resistance, which helps build muscle strength and endurance.
- *Enhanced Posture and Alignment:*
  - Posture: *Asanas* promote awareness of body alignment and help correct poor posture, which can prevent back and neck pain.
  - Spinal Health: Yoga poses such as twists and backbends strengthen the spine and improve overall spinal health.
- *Better Balance and Coordination:*
  - Balance: Practicing poses that challenge balance helps improve stability and coordination, which is particularly beneficial as women age.
  - Proprioception: Enhanced body awareness can improve coordination and reduce the risk of falls.
- *Improved Circulation and Cardiovascular Health:*
  - Blood Flow: *Asanas* promote better circulation, ensuring that oxygen and nutrients are efficiently delivered to cells.
  - Heart Health: Certain yoga practices can help lower blood pressure and improve heart rate variability, benefiting cardiovascular health.
- *Enhanced Digestive Health:*
  - Digestion: Poses that involve twisting and compression can stimulate digestive organs, improving digestion and relieving issues like constipation and bloating.
- *Hormonal Balance:*
  - Endocrine System: Yoga can help regulate the endocrine system, aiding in hormonal balance which is crucial during menstruation, pregnancy, and menopause.

Mental and Emotional Benefits

- *Stress Reduction:*
  - Relaxation: *Pranayama* techniques like deep breathing and alternate nostril breathing activate the parasympathetic nervous system, reducing stress and promoting relaxation.
  - Mindfulness: Yoga encourages mindfulness and presence, which can help women manage stress more effectively.
- *Improved Focus and Concentration:*
  - Mental Clarity: The practice of focusing on breath and movement enhances mental clarity and concentration, aiding in better decision-making and productivity.
- *Emotional Stability:*
  - Emotional Regulation: Regular practice helps in managing emotions, reducing mood swings, and promoting a sense of emotional stability.
- *Anxiety and Depression Relief:*
  - Calming Effects: Certain *pranayama* techniques and restorative *asanas* can help alleviate symptoms of anxiety and depression by calming the mind and balancing the nervous system.

Benefits Specific to Women's Health

- *Menstrual Health:*
  - Menstrual Relief: Yoga can help alleviate menstrual discomfort, cramps, and PMS symptoms through poses that relieve tension and promote relaxation.
  - Cycle Regulation: Regular practice can help regulate menstrual cycles and reduce the severity of symptoms associated with hormonal imbalances.
- *Pregnancy and Postpartum Health:*
  - Prenatal Yoga: Helps prepare the body for childbirth by improving strength, flexibility, and endurance. It also aids in managing pregnancy-related discomforts.
  - Postpartum Recovery: Postnatal yoga supports recovery after childbirth, helping to strengthen the pelvic floor, reduce back pain, and promote emotional well-being.
- *Menopausal Support:*
  - Symptom Relief: Yoga can help manage menopausal symptoms such as hot flashes, mood swings, and sleep disturbances by promoting relaxation and hormonal balance.

- Bone Health: Weight-bearing *asanas* help maintain bone density, reducing the risk of osteoporosis.

Social and Spiritual Benefits

- *Community and Connection:*
  - Social Interaction: Attending yoga classes provides an opportunity for social interaction and building a supportive community.
  - Shared Experiences: Women can share experiences and support each other through various life stages, from menstruation to menopause.
- *Spiritual Growth:*
  - Inner Peace: The combination of *asanas* and *pranayama* promotes a sense of inner peace and connection to oneself, aiding in spiritual growth.
  - Mind-Body Connection: Yoga fosters a deeper connection between mind and body, enhancing overall self-awareness and spiritual well-being.

Practicing *Asana* and *Pranayama* offers a holistic approach to health and well-being for women. These practices not only enhance physical strength, flexibility, and posture but also promote mental clarity, emotional stability, and hormonal balance. By integrating yoga into their daily lives, women can experience significant improvements in their overall quality of life, from managing stress and anxiety to supporting reproductive health and fostering a sense of community and spiritual growth. The benefits of yoga are far-reaching and can provide a strong foundation for a healthy, balanced, and fulfilling life.

8

Yoga at Work Place

Offices and Corporate Sector

Employee satisfaction leads to a positive ambience at the workplace. Satisfied employees feel more invested in a company's success and therefore work harder to help achieve it. Employees who are satisfied with their jobs tend to be more productive. The aim should be to create a culture of well-being within the workplace, where employees prioritise self-care and make use of the available tools to alleviate stress and enhance their overall work experience.

Corporate employees spend most of their time sitting in chairs for long hours, hunched over their computers. Unaware of it, this unnatural position is detrimental to their health, causing back and neck pain, which can further hamper their productivity. In fact, back pain is one of the main reasons people take up yoga. Yoga helps relieve pain through its stretches and poses, targeting major muscle groups to increase flexibility and prevent stiffness and joint aches. A stressful corporate life with tight deadlines, heavy workloads, and endless meetings can create mental clutter, hindering employees' decision-making and ability to concentrate on tasks.

Yoga poses and meditation help clear this mental clutter, making employees more alert, focused, and productive. Improved blood circulation in the brain enhances brain function, while yoga and meditation teach employees to maintain a still and focused mind—an invaluable skill in a demanding work environment. Workplace stress causes frustration and anger, leading to decreased motivation and productivity. When employees are physically and mentally unwell, their morale suffers.

Yoga's stress reduction properties elevate employees' mood and keep anger at bay, improving mental and physical health, and helping them stay motivated and confident. By boosting morale, yoga creates a harmonious workplace. Conducting yoga classes for employees promotes its health benefits and fosters a healthy workforce.

Yoga increases focus and concentration among employees, making them more productive. With increased concentration and better focus, creativity also follows. Not only does office yoga give a boost of energy, but it can prevent a burnout feeling.

Practicing regular yoga supports and broadens creative expression. It refines inner emotions, balancing the mind, body, and soul. This results in a clear animation of creative expression in an employee, helping him complete tasks creatively and innovatively.

Yoga benefits not only the physical health of your employees but also benefits your workplace in many ways. Yoga increases energy levels and boosts employee morale, making them more productive in their work.

Also, when your employees are free of any kind of pain or health problems, they will be present more often, attentive, focused, and productive.

Doing yoga in the office can be fun, innovative and relaxing with many long term benefits. Prolonged work on the computer strains the neck, shoulder and back muscles, which leads to tension and stiffness. Unless attended to properly, it could impact your ability to function effectively at the workplace, affecting your overall quality of life. Office yoga comprises a sequence of simple exercises you can perform quite unobtrusively at your desk, at any time of the day.

Making corporate yoga exercises a part of your routine can work wonders as they wipe away body pain, fatigue and tension and increase overall muscle strength and flexibility, keeping you fresh and revitalised throughout the day. The exercises don't demand much time, and can be done in spurts throughout the day, sparing you from unnecessary discomfort in the long run.

Challenges of Work Place for Employees

The Indian workplace has undergone significant transformations over the past few decades, driven by globalisation, technological advancements, and socio-economic changes. While these developments have opened up new opportunities, they have also introduced a unique set of challenges for employees. Understanding these challenges is crucial for fostering a productive and supportive work environment.

Work-Life Balance

One of the most pressing issues for Indian employees is maintaining a healthy work-life balance. The traditional expectation of long working hours, often exacerbated by the demands of multinational companies, leaves little time for personal and family life. The pressure to perform and the fear of job insecurity can lead to burnout, adversely affecting mental and physical health.

Workplace Culture and Hierarchy

The hierarchical nature of many Indian workplaces can pose challenges. Employees often face rigid structures and power dynamics that limit open communication and innovation. The cultural emphasis on respect for authority can sometimes stifle creativity and discourage younger employees from voicing their ideas or concerns.

Gender Disparity and Inclusivity

Despite progress in gender equality, significant disparities remain in Indian workplaces. Women often face challenges related to equal pay, career advancement, and work-life balance. Additionally, workplace harassment and the lack of adequate support systems can hinder their professional growth. Inclusivity issues also extend to other marginalised groups, such as LGBTQ+ individuals and people with disabilities, who may encounter biases and lack of appropriate accommodations.

Skill Development and Training

The rapid pace of technological change necessitates continuous skill development. However, many Indian companies lag in providing adequate training and development programmes. Employees often struggle to keep up with new technologies and methodologies, which can lead to job dissatisfaction and reduced productivity. There is a growing need for organisations to invest in reskilling and upskilling their workforce.

Mental Health Awareness

Mental health is a critical yet often overlooked aspect of employee well-being in India. The stigma surrounding mental health issues can prevent employees from seeking help. High stress levels, unrealistic performance expectations, and a lack of supportive workplace policies can exacerbate mental health problems. Employers need to create environments where mental health is openly discussed and supported.

Remote Work and Technological Challenges

The COVID-19 pandemic has accelerated the shift to remote work, bringing its own set of challenges. Many employees face issues related to inadequate infrastructure, such as poor internet connectivity and lack of proper workspaces at home. Additionally, the blurred boundaries between work and personal life can increase stress and reduce productivity. Companies need to provide the necessary tools and support to ensure a smooth transition to remote work.

Job Security and Contract Work

Job security is a major concern for many Indian employees. The emergence of the gig economy and contract work has brought flexibility but it has also heightened uncertainty. Contract workers often lack the benefits and protections afforded to full-time employees, such as health insurance, paid leave, and job stability. This can lead to financial insecurity and anxiety.

Employee Engagement and Motivation

Maintaining high levels of employee engagement and motivation is an ongoing challenge. Factors such as monotonous tasks, lack of recognition, and limited career growth opportunities can lead to disengagement. Employers need to implement strategies that foster a sense of purpose, provide meaningful work, and recognise and reward employee contributions.

Compliance with Labour Laws

Navigating the complex landscape of labour laws and regulations in India can be daunting for both employers and employees. Frequent changes in legislation, coupled with variations across states, create confusion and compliance challenges. Ensuring that employees are aware of their rights and that companies adhere to legal requirements is essential for a fair and just workplace.

Health and Safety Concerns

Health and safety in the workplace are paramount, yet many Indian workplaces fall short in this area. Employees in certain industries, such as manufacturing and construction, are particularly vulnerable to accidents and occupational hazards. Ensuring proper safety measures, training, and compliance with health regulations is crucial to protect employees' well-being.

Addressing the challenges faced by employees in the Indian workplace requires a multifaceted approach. Employers must recognise the evolving needs of their workforce and implement policies that promote work-life balance, inclusivity, and continuous learning. By fostering a supportive and engaging work environment, companies can enhance employee satisfaction, productivity, and overall well-being. It is only through such concerted efforts that the Indian workplace can truly thrive in the modern era.

Yoga's Role in Coping Challenges

Yoga, with its holistic approach to physical and mental well-being, can be a powerful tool for addressing many of the challenges faced by employees in the modern workplace. Here's how yoga can play a significant role in coping with the challenges mentioned:

Work-Life Balance

Stress Reduction: Yoga incorporates relaxation techniques and mindfulness practices that help reduce stress. Regular practice of yoga can lower cortisol levels, making it easier for employees to manage stress and maintain a healthier work-life balance.

Enhanced Focus: Mindfulness and meditation practices within yoga can help employees stay present and focused, which can improve efficiency and reduce the spill over of work-related stress into personal life.

Workplace Culture and Hierarchy

Improved Communication: Yoga promotes self-awareness and empathy, which can enhance interpersonal relationships and communication in the workplace. This helps in breaking down hierarchical barriers and fosters a more inclusive and collaborative environment.

Emotional Intelligence: Yoga can improve emotional intelligence, enabling employees to navigate workplace dynamics more effectively and respond to challenges with a calm and balanced approach.

Gender Disparity and Inclusivity

Empowerment: Yoga can boost self-confidence and self-awareness, helping women and marginalised groups to assert themselves more confidently in the workplace.

Supportive Environment: Organisations that promote yoga and wellness programs demonstrate a commitment to the well-being of all employees, contributing to a more inclusive and supportive workplace culture.

Skill Development and Training

Enhanced Focus and Learning: Yoga practices that improve concentration and mental clarity can enhance the ability to learn new skills and adapt to changing technological landscapes.

Resilience: Yoga builds mental and physical resilience, helping employees stay motivated and engaged in continuous learning and development.

Mental Health Awareness

Anxiety and Depression Management: Yoga has been shown to alleviate symptoms of anxiety and depression, promoting overall mental well-being. Regular practice can help employees manage workplace stress and mental health issues more effectively.

Creating a Supportive Culture: Promoting yoga and mindfulness can help destigmatise mental health issues, encouraging employees to seek help and support when needed.

Remote Work and Technological Challenges

Physical Well-being: Yoga addresses the physical strain caused by prolonged sitting and poor posture, common in remote work setups. Practicing yoga can alleviate back pain, neck strain, and other musculoskeletal issues.

Mental Clarity: Yoga and meditation can improve mental clarity and focus, helping remote workers maintain productivity and manage the blurred boundaries between work and personal life.

Job Security and Contract Work

Stress Management: Yoga provides tools for managing stress and anxiety associated with job insecurity and financial instability. Practices like deep breathing and meditation can help individuals remain calm and composed during uncertain times.

Resilience and Adaptability: Yoga enhances resilience and adaptability, equipping employees with the mental strength to cope with the uncertainties of contract work and the gig economy.

Employee Engagement and Motivation

Energy Boost: Yoga can increase energy levels and reduce fatigue, leading to higher engagement and motivation at work. A revitalised workforce is more likely to be productive and creative.

Sense of Purpose: Yoga encourages self-reflection and mindfulness, helping employees connect with their inner purpose and find meaning in their work.

Compliance with Labour Laws

Awareness and Advocacy: Yoga practices that promote mindfulness and self-awareness can encourage employees to be more aware of their rights and advocate for themselves and others in the workplace.

Holistic Well-being: Companies that integrate yoga into their wellness programmes demonstrate a commitment to holistic well-being, which includes adhering to labour laws and promoting fair treatment.

Health and Safety Concerns

Preventive Care: Yoga promotes physical fitness and flexibility, reducing the risk of workplace injuries and occupational hazards. Regular practice can prevent common health issues like repetitive strain injuries.

Safety Culture: A culture that values yoga and wellness is likely to prioritise health and safety, creating a safer and healthier work environment for all employees.

Integrating yoga into the workplace can be a powerful strategy to address the multifaceted challenges faced by employees in India. By promoting physical, mental, and emotional well-being, yoga can enhance overall employee satisfaction, productivity, and resilience. Employers who invest in yoga and wellness programmes not only support their employees' health but also contribute to creating a more positive, inclusive, and thriving workplace culture.

Integrating Yoga in Corporate Offices

Employee well-being and productivity. Initially, it's essential to assess employee interest through surveys and focus groups to tailor the programme effectively. Securing management support by presenting the benefits of yoga, such as stress reduction and improved mental health, is crucial for garnering resources and commitment. Designating a suitable, quiet space equipped with basic yoga necessities creates an inviting environment. Hiring certified instructors to lead regular, varied sessions ensures professional guidance and caters to different fitness levels and preferences. Scheduling classes at convenient times, promoting participation through internal marketing and incentives, and integrating mindfulness practices like meditation and breathing exercises further embed yoga into the daily routine. Regular feedback and evaluation help in refining the programme, while leadership participation fosters a culture of wellness. By adopting these steps, companies can seamlessly incorporate yoga, leading to a healthier, more engaged workforce.

Benefits

Incorporating yoga into the corporate environment offers substantial benefits to both the organisation and its employees, starting with enhanced physical health. Regular yoga practice helps employees manage the physical strains of prolonged sitting and poor posture common in office settings. It alleviates issues such as back pain, neck strain, and repetitive stress injuries. Improved physical health reduces absenteeism and healthcare costs, contributing to a more efficient and resilient workforce. For corporations, this translates into reduced medical expenses and fewer lost workdays, ultimately boosting overall productivity and workplace morale.

Yoga also significantly improves mental well-being, which is crucial in high-pressure corporate environments. Practices such as meditation and deep breathing exercises help reduce stress and anxiety, promoting mental clarity and emotional stability. Employees who regularly practice yoga are likely to experience better focus, creativity, and problem-solving skills. This mental resilience enables them to handle work-related challenges more effectively and maintain a positive outlook. For the corporation, a mentally healthy workforce means enhanced productivity, lower turnover rates, and a more innovative and dynamic work environment.

Beyond individual benefits, yoga fosters a sense of community and teamwork within the corporate setting. Group yoga sessions encourage social interaction and teamwork, strengthening relationships among employees across different departments. This camaraderie improves communication, collaboration, and a sense of belonging, which are vital for a cohesive and motivated workforce. By promoting yoga and wellness programs, corporations demonstrate a commitment to their employees' well-being, which can enhance job satisfaction, loyalty, and overall organizational culture. A positive work environment not only attracts top talent but also ensures that employees are engaged, motivated, and committed to the company's success.

9

Yoga for Sports and Atheletics

The life of a sportsperson is often perceived as glamorous, filled with fame and fortune. However, behind the scenes, athletes face numerous challenges that test their physical, mental, and emotional resilience. These challenges, although daunting, are part and parcel of their journey to excellence.

Challenges being Faced

Physical Demands and Injuries

One of the most significant challenges for any sportsperson is the intense physical demands of training and competition. Athletes undergo rigorous training regimens, often pushing their bodies to the limits. This constant strain can result in overuse injuries, which are common in sports. Injuries not only cause physical pain but also interrupt training schedules and competition timelines, potentially derailing an athlete's career. Recovering from injuries requires time, patience, and often extensive rehabilitation, during which athletes may experience anxiety about their return to peak performance.

Mental Health and Pressure

The pressure to perform at the highest level can take a severe toll on a sportsperson's mental health. The constant need to win, meet expectations from coaches, sponsors, fans, and even personal goals can lead to immense stress. Additionally, the fear of failure and the scrutiny from media and the public can cause anxiety and depression. Maintaining mental well-being amidst such pressures is challenging. Athletes must find a balance between their competitive drive and mental health, often requiring professional psychological support.

Work-Life Balance

Balancing professional commitments with personal life is a significant challenge for sportspeople. The demanding nature of sports often requires extensive travel, long hours of practice, and strict dietary and sleep schedules. This can strain personal relationships and family life. Many athletes struggle to maintain healthy relationships and miss out on important life events. The lack of time for relaxation and personal pursuits can lead to burnout, affecting both their performance and overall well-being.

Financial Uncertainty

Contrary to popular belief, not all athletes enjoy financial stability. While top-tier athletes in certain sports earn substantial incomes, many others struggle with financial insecurity. The cost of training, equipment, travel, and medical expenses can be overwhelming, especially for those who are not sponsored or are in the early stages of their careers. Financial pressure can add to the stress of performing well and securing future contracts or sponsorships.

Transitioning and Career Longevity

The career span of a sportsperson is often limited due to the physical demands of their profession. Planning for life after sports is a critical yet challenging aspect. Athletes must consider education, alternative career paths, and financial planning for their post-retirement life. The transition from an active sports career to retirement can be emotionally challenging as well, as many athletes struggle with identity loss and finding a new purpose.

Handling Public Scrutiny and Media

Athletes are often in the public eye, and their actions, both on and off the field, are scrutinised. Handling media pressure and maintaining a positive public image is a constant challenge. Negative publicity, criticism, or scandals can severely impact an athlete's career and mental health. Managing social media presence and dealing with cyberbullying are relatively new challenges that modern athletes face.

Access to Resources

Access to quality training facilities, coaching, and medical care is not consistent across all regions and sports. Athletes from developing countries or less popular sports often face challenges in accessing these critical resources. This disparity can hinder their development and limit their potential. Equal opportunities and investment in sports infrastructure are essential to overcome these challenges.

The life of a sportsperson, while rewarding, is fraught with numerous challenges. Overcoming physical injuries, managing mental health, maintaining work-life balance, ensuring financial stability, planning for the future, handling public scrutiny, and accessing resources are all significant hurdles. However, the resilience and determination required to face these challenges contribute to the incredible achievements and inspiring stories of athletes worldwide. Recognising and addressing these challenges is crucial for the holistic development and support of sportspeople.

How Yoga can Play a Significant Role in Coping with these Challenges

Yoga offers a comprehensive approach to addressing the multifaceted challenges faced by sportspersons, providing physical, mental, and emotional benefits that are crucial for their well-being and performance. Here's how yoga can play a significant role in coping with these challenges:

Physical Demands and Injuries

Injury Prevention and Rehabilitation: Yoga promotes flexibility, strength, and balance, which are essential for preventing injuries common in sports. Specific yoga poses and sequences can target areas prone to injury, such as hamstrings, shoulders, and lower back. Additionally, yoga enhances body awareness, allowing athletes to recognise early signs of strain and adjust their training accordingly. For athletes recovering from injuries, gentle yoga practices can facilitate rehabilitation by improving circulation, reducing stiffness, and promoting healing.

Mental Health and Pressure

Stress Reduction: Yoga includes techniques such as deep breathing (*pranayama*) and meditation that promote relaxation and reduce stress levels. These practices activate the parasympathetic nervous system, leading to a calmer state of mind. Regular yoga sessions provide athletes with valuable time to unwind, release tension, and regain mental clarity amidst the pressures of competition and expectations.

Mindfulness and Focus: Yoga cultivates mindfulness, enhancing athletes' ability to stay present and focused during training and competition. By practicing mindfulness techniques on the mat, athletes can apply these skills to maintain concentration, manage distractions, and perform at their peak under pressure.

Work-Life Balance

Integration of Body and Mind: Yoga emphasises the integration of physical movement with mental awareness and relaxation. Athletes can use yoga sessions as a holistic approach to self-care, balancing the intense physical demands of training with mental rejuvenation. This balance extends beyond the mat, helping athletes maintain harmony between their professional and personal lives.

Financial Uncertainty

Stress Management: Yoga offers tools for managing stress related to financial pressures and career uncertainties. Breathing exercises and mindfulness practices can help athletes cultivate resilience, maintain a positive mindset, and make informed decisions about their financial future.

Transitioning and Career Longevity

Self-Reflection and Goal Setting: Yoga promotes self-reflection and introspection, supporting athletes in navigating career transitions. Through yoga, athletes can explore new passions, set meaningful goals, and develop resilience to adapt to life changes beyond their sports careers.

Handling Public Scrutiny and Media

Emotional Resilience: Yoga enhances emotional resilience, helping athletes manage criticism, public scrutiny, and the pressures of maintaining a positive public image. By fostering inner strength and self-confidence, yoga empowers athletes to stay grounded and focused on their personal and professional values.

Access to Resources

Accessibility and Adaptability: Yoga is accessible to athletes of all levels and can be practiced virtually anywhere, requiring minimal equipment. Athletes from diverse backgrounds and regions can benefit from yoga's adaptability, regardless of access to traditional training facilities or resources.

Yoga serves as a powerful tool for sportspersons to enhance their overall well-being, resilience, and performance. By integrating yoga into their training routines, athletes can effectively manage physical demands, reduce stress, maintain mental clarity, and cultivate a balanced lifestyle. The holistic benefits of yoga extend beyond physical fitness, supporting athletes in navigating the challenges of their careers and achieving sustainable success both on and off the field.

What should be the Government Policy for the Sports Person?

Government policies for sports persons should encompass a comprehensive approach that supports athletes throughout their careers, promotes sports participation and excellence, ensures equitable opportunities, and enhances sports infrastructure. Here are key components that should be considered in formulating effective government policies for sports persons:

Financial Support and Incentives

Grants and Scholarships: Provide financial support through grants, scholarships, and stipends to athletes at various levels of their careers. This support should cover training expenses, equipment, travel costs for competitions, and living expenses.

Insurance and Medical Coverage: Ensure comprehensive health insurance coverage and access to quality medical care, including sports-specific rehabilitation services. Athletes should be protected against career-ending injuries and provided with necessary support for recovery.

Tax Incentives: Introduce tax incentives for sports persons and sports-related organisations to encourage investment in sports development and athlete welfare.

Infrastructure Development

Sports Facilities: Invest in the development and maintenance of state-of-the-art sports facilities across regions, ensuring accessibility for athletes of all backgrounds. This includes training centers, stadiums, swimming pools, tracks, and gyms equipped with modern amenities.

Sports Science and Technology: Promote research and development in sports science, nutrition, biomechanics, and sports technology. Establish sports research institutes and laboratories to support evidence-based training and performance enhancement.

Education and Career Development

Dual Career Pathways: Support athletes in balancing sports careers with education or vocational training. Implement flexible academic programs, scholarships for athletes pursuing higher education, and career counseling services.

Post-Retirement Planning: Provide resources and guidance for athletes to plan for life after retirement from sports, including entrepreneurship opportunities, job placement services, and financial literacy programs.

Coach and Official Development

Training and Certification: Establish programmes for training and certifying coaches, sports officials, and sports administrators. Ensure continuous professional development opportunities to maintain high standards of coaching and officiating.

Incentives for Coaches: Provide incentives and recognition for coaches who demonstrate excellence in developing athletes and achieving competitive success at national and international levels.

Promotion of Sports Culture and Participation

School and Community Programmes: Integrate sports into school curricula and community programmes to promote grassroots participation from a young age. Provide incentives for schools and local authorities to develop sports infrastructure and organize competitions.

Sports Events and Festivals: Support the organisation of national and international sports events, championships, and cultural festivals to showcase talent, foster national pride, and attract tourism.

Governance and Anti-Doping Measures

Transparency and Accountability: Ensure transparent governance structures in sports organizations, promoting integrity and fair play. Implement measures to prevent corruption, doping, and unethical practices in sports.

Anti-Doping Policies: Enforce stringent anti-doping policies and programmes to protect the integrity of sports and ensure a level playing field for athletes. Educate athletes and stakeholders on anti-doping regulations and consequences of doping violations.

Inclusion and Diversity

Gender Equality: Promote gender equality in sports by providing equal opportunities, resources, and recognition for female athletes.

Address barriers to women's participation and leadership in sports organisations.

Inclusion of Persons with Disabilities: Support the participation of persons with disabilities in sports through inclusive policies, accessible facilities, adaptive equipment, and specialised training programs.

Effective government policies for sports persons should be inclusive, sustainable, and aimed at nurturing a vibrant sports ecosystem. By prioritising financial support, infrastructure development, education, career development, coaching excellence, anti-doping measures, and promoting sports culture, governments can empower athletes to excel both on and off the field. Investing in sports not only enhances national competitiveness in international arenas but also contributes to the overall health, well-being, and unity of society.

10

Yoga for Defence Personnel

Defence personnel serving in border security forces and the Indian Army face unique and daunting challenges due to the diverse geographical locations and harsh climates they operate in. These challenges significantly impact their operational effectiveness, physical health, and mental well-being.

Challenges Impacting Operational Effectiveness, Physical Health and Mental Well-being

Extreme Weather Conditions

Defense personnel often operate in regions with extreme weather conditions, ranging from scorching heat in deserts to freezing temperatures in high-altitude mountainous regions. These conditions pose significant risks such as heat strokes, frostbite, hypothermia, and dehydration. Maintaining physical endurance and operational readiness becomes challenging when soldiers must endure prolonged exposure to these harsh environments.

Terrain and Geographical Challenges

The diverse terrain across India's borders presents formidable challenges to defence personnel. They may be deployed in dense forests, rugged mountains, barren deserts, or swampy marshlands. Navigating through such varied terrain requires specialised training and equipment. Movement and communication can be hindered by natural obstacles like rivers, cliffs, and thick vegetation, impacting operational efficiency and response times.

Isolation and Limited Infrastructure

Many border posts and military bases are located in remote and isolated areas with limited infrastructure and connectivity. Access to basic amenities such as clean water, medical facilities, and adequate housing can be scarce. This isolation adds to the psychological stress and sense of detachment from civilian life for soldiers who may spend extended periods away from their families and support networks.

Security Threats and Border Management

Border security forces and the Indian Army are tasked with safeguarding India's borders against various security threats, including infiltration, smuggling, and terrorist activities. Operating in volatile border regions requires constant vigilance and readiness to respond swiftly to any security breaches. The unpredictable nature of these threats adds to the stress and mental burden on defence personnel.

Psychological and Emotional Stress

The demanding nature of their duties, coupled with the inherent risks and hardships, can lead to significant psychological and emotional stress among defence personnel. Witnessing combat situations, experiencing casualties within their units, and living under constant threat impact soldiers' mental well-being. Post-traumatic stress disorder (PTSD), anxiety, and depression are prevalent among military personnel deployed in conflict zones or high-stress environments.

Family Separation and Personal Sacrifices

Deployments often require defence personnel to be away from their families for extended periods, sometimes in remote and dangerous locations. This separation can strain family relationships, cause emotional distress, and affect the well-being of both soldiers and their loved ones. Balancing the demands of duty with personal responsibilities and maintaining morale becomes a constant challenge.

High Physical Demands and Health Risks

The rigorous training and operational demands placed on defence personnel require them to maintain peak physical fitness and endurance. Long patrols, carrying heavy equipment, and engaging in physically demanding tasks take a toll on their bodies. Injuries, fatigue, and exhaustion are common, particularly during extended deployments in challenging environments.

Defence personnel serving in border security forces and the Indian Army confront a myriad of challenges related to geographical locations, harsh climates, security threats, psychological stress, and personal sacrifices. Addressing these challenges requires comprehensive support systems, including adequate training, specialised equipment, infrastructure development, and robust healthcare services. Recognising and mitigating these challenges is essential to ensuring the well-being and operational effectiveness of the brave men and women who serve on India's borders.

Effect of Implimenting of Yoga in their Lifestyle

The integration of yoga into the routine of defence personnel serving in border security forces and the Indian Army can have profound effects on their physical health, mental well-being, and overall operational readiness. Here's how yoga can positively impact their lives:

Physical Benefits

- *Flexibility and Strength:* Yoga practices such as *asanas* (poses) and stretching exercises enhance flexibility and improve muscle strength. This is crucial for soldiers who often face physically demanding tasks and need to maintain agility and endurance across varied terrains and climates.
- *Injury Prevention and Rehabilitation:* Yoga promotes body awareness and corrects imbalances, reducing the risk of injuries during training and operations. For those recovering from injuries, yoga can aid in rehabilitation by gently restoring mobility and strength without exacerbating existing conditions.
- *Stamina and Endurance:* Breathing techniques (*pranayama*) practiced in yoga help improve respiratory efficiency and increase lung capacity, which is beneficial in coping with high-altitude environments and prolonged physical exertion.

2. Mental and Emotional Well-being

- *Stress Reduction:* Yoga techniques such as deep breathing, meditation, and mindfulness promote relaxation and reduce stress levels. Soldiers facing high-pressure situations and constant vigilance can benefit from these practices to maintain emotional stability and mental clarity.
- *Focus and Concentration:* Yoga enhances mental focus and concentration through meditation and mindfulness practices. Improved focus is crucial for maintaining situational awareness, making quick decisions, and executing tasks effectively in challenging and unpredictable environments.
- *Emotional Resilience:* Regular yoga practice fosters emotional resilience, helping soldiers cope with the psychological stresses of combat, isolation, and prolonged deployments. It provides them with tools to manage anxiety, fear, and uncertainty, promoting a balanced state of mind even amidst adversity.

3. Overall Well-being and Morale

- *Holistic Health:* Yoga promotes holistic well-being by addressing physical, mental, and emotional aspects of health. It encourages a balanced lifestyle, healthy habits, and self-care practices that contribute to overall wellness and resilience.
- *Team Building and Camaraderie:* Group yoga sessions can foster camaraderie and teamwork among soldiers, enhancing unit cohesion and morale. Practicing together creates a supportive environment where individuals can bond over shared experiences and mutual respect.

4. Practical Application in Military Operations

- *Adaptability and Versatility:* Yoga's adaptability makes it suitable for various operational contexts, whether soldiers are deployed in remote outposts or engaged in active combat. Practices can be modified to accommodate different physical abilities and environmental conditions.
- *Quick Recovery and Readiness:* Yoga's emphasis on relaxation and rejuvenation can aid in quicker recovery after strenuous missions or physical exertion. Soldiers can restore their energy levels and readiness faster, ensuring they are prepared for subsequent tasks and challenges.

Integrating yoga into the routine of defence personnel offers numerous benefits that enhance their physical capabilities, mental resilience, and overall well-being. By incorporating yoga practices tailored to the unique demands of military life, such as flexibility, strength, stress reduction, and emotional balance, soldiers can better cope with the rigors of their duties. Yoga not only supports individual health but also contributes to unit cohesion and operational effectiveness, ultimately strengthening the readiness and effectiveness of India's defence forces.

Tailored Yoga Practice for Defence Persons

Designing a tailored yoga practice for defence personnel should focus on enhancing physical strength, flexibility, mental resilience, and stress management. This practice should be adaptable to different fitness levels and operational environments. Here's a structured yoga routine specifically for Defence Personnel:

Warm-Up (5 minutes)

1. Neck Rolls:
    - Stand or sit comfortably.
    - Slowly rotate the neck clockwise and then counter clockwise.

- Repeat 5 times in each direction to release tension in the neck and shoulders.

2. Shoulder Rolls:
    - Roll the shoulders forward and backward in a smooth motion.
    - Repeat 10 times in each direction to loosen up the shoulder joints.
3. Gentle Spinal Twist:
    - Sit on the floor or chair with a straight spine.
    - Inhale to lengthen the spine, then exhale to twist gently to the right.
    - Hold for a few breaths, then switch sides.
    - Repeat 2–3 times on each side to warm up the spine and improve mobility.

Main Practice (20–30 minutes)

1. *Standing Poses for Strength and Stability:*
    a. Warrior Poses (*Virabhadrasana* I and II):
        - Strengthen legs, core, and improve balance.
        - Hold each pose for 5–8 breaths.
        - Repeat on both sides.

    b. Chair Pose (*Utkatasana*):
        - Stand with feet hip-width apart, arms overhead.
        - Bend knees and lower hips as if sitting in a chair.
        - Hold for 5–8 breaths to build strength in legs and core.
2. *Core Strengthening:*
    a. Plank Pose:
        - Come into a push-up position with wrists under shoulders.
        - Engage core and legs, keep the body in a straight line.
        - Hold for 30 seconds to 1 minute, or as long as comfortable.

    b. Boat Pose (*Navasana*):
        - Sit on the floor, lift legs to a 45-degree angle from the ground.
        - Extend arms parallel to the floor.
        - Hold for 5–8 breaths to strengthen core muscles.
3. *Flexibility and Mobility:*
    a. Forward Fold (*Uttanasana*):
        - Stand with feet hip-width apart, fold forward from hips.
        - Relax head and neck, reaching hands towards the ground or legs.
        - Hold for 5–8 breaths to stretch hamstrings and release tension in the back.

    b. Seated Forward Bend (*Paschimottanasana*):
        - Sit with legs extended, feet flexed.
        - Inhale to lengthen the spine, exhale to fold forward from hips.
        - Hold onto feet or legs, keeping the back straight.
        - Hold for 5–8 breaths to stretch hamstrings and improve flexibility.

Cool Down and Relaxation (5–10 minutes)

1. Reclining Spinal Twist:
   - Lie on the back, bend knees towards the chest.
   - Lower legs to one side, extend arms out in a T position.
   - Hold for 5–8 breaths on each side to release tension in the spine.
2. Corpse Pose (*Savasana*):
   - Lie on the back with legs extended, arms by the sides.
   - Close eyes and relax completely, focusing on deep breathing.
   - Remain in *Savasana* for 5–10 minutes to allow the body and mind to integrate the benefits of the practice.

Pranayama (Breathing Exercises)

1. Equal Breathing (*Sama Vritti*):
   - Sit comfortably, close eyes.
   - Inhale for a count of 4, exhale for a count of 4.
   - Repeat for 5–10 cycles to calm the mind and regulate breathing.
2. Three-Part Breath (*Dirga Pranayama*):
   - Sit or lie down comfortably.
   - Inhale deeply into the belly, then expand the rib cage and finally fill the chest.
   - Exhale slowly, reversing the process.
   - Repeat for 5–10 cycles to increase lung capacity and relaxation.

This tailored yoga practice for defense personnel aims to improve physical strength, flexibility, mental resilience, and stress management. It provides a structured sequence of poses, breathing exercises, and relaxation techniques that can be practiced regularly to support overall health and well-being in demanding military environments. Adjustments can be made based on individual fitness levels and specific operational requirements. Regular practice of yoga can help defence personnel maintain optimal physical and mental readiness for their duties.

The tailored yoga practices provide defence personnel with a comprehensive toolkit to enhance their physical strength, mental resilience, and emotional well-being in demanding military environments. By integrating these practices into their routine, soldiers can improve their overall health, manage stress effectively, prevent injuries, and maintain peak performance during operations. These benefits not only support individual soldiers but also contribute to the cohesive and effective functioning of military units, ultimately enhancing national defence capabilities.

11

Yoga for Personality Development

Personality is a complex and multifaceted aspect of human psychology that encompasses the patterns of thoughts, feelings, and behaviours that distinguish individuals from one another. It is the unique combination of traits, characteristics, and temperament that defines how we perceive the world, interact with others, and navigate through life's challenges.

Understanding Personality

At its core, personality represents the stable and enduring qualities that shape an individual's responses to various situations and influences. It is influenced by genetic predispositions, early life experiences, social and cultural factors, and on-going interactions with the environment. While genetics provide a foundational blueprint, environmental factors play a significant role in shaping and refining personality over time.

Components of Personality

- *Traits:* Personality traits are enduring patterns of behaviour, thoughts, and emotions that are relatively consistent across different situations. Traits can range from introversion to extraversion, agreeableness to hostility, conscientiousness to impulsiveness, openness to experience, and emotional stability.
- *Temperament:* Temperament refers to innate, biologically based tendencies that influence an individual's approach to and interaction with the world. It includes aspects such as sensitivity to stimuli, adaptability, activity level, and emotional reactivity, which are observable from early childhood.
- *Character:* Character encompasses moral and ethical dimensions of personality, reflecting a person's values, beliefs, and integrity. It involves traits such as honesty, integrity, empathy, and responsibility, which guide ethical decision-making and behaviour.

- *Cognitive and Emotional Patterns*: Cognitive and emotional patterns refer to the ways individuals process information, perceive events, and regulate their emotions. These patterns influence how people interpret experiences, manage stress, and form relationships.

Theories of Personality

- *Trait Theories:* Trait theories of personality emphasize identifying and categorising stable patterns of behaviour. Psychologists such as Gordon Allport and Raymond Cattell developed trait models that classify personality traits into distinct categories, facilitating understanding of individual differences.
- *Psychodynamic Theories:* Psychodynamic theories, notably Sigmund Freud's psychoanalytic theory and later developments by Carl Jung and Erik Erikson, focus on unconscious processes, childhood experiences, and internal conflicts that shape personality development. These theories emphasise the role of unconscious desires and defence mechanisms in shaping behaviour.
- *Humanistic Theories:* Humanistic theories, including Abraham Maslow's hierarchy of needs and Carl Rogers' person-centred theory, emphasise personal growth, self-actualisation, and the innate drive towards fulfilling one's potential. These theories highlight the importance of self-awareness, self-acceptance, and authenticity in shaping personality.
- *Behavioural and Social-Cognitive Theories:* Behavioural and social-cognitive theories focus on how external influences, learning experiences, and social interactions shape personality development. Albert Bandura's social-cognitive theory emphasises observational learning, self-efficacy, and the role of cognitive processes in shaping behaviour.

Importance of Personality

Personality plays a pivotal role in various aspects of life, influencing career choices, interpersonal relationships, coping strategies, and overall well-being. A person's personality traits and characteristics impact their leadership style, communication preferences, decision-making abilities, and responses to stress and adversity.

Understanding personality is essential for self-awareness and personal growth, enabling individuals to recognise their strengths, areas for development, and potential impact on others. It informs psychological assessments, counselling interventions, and organisational strategies aimed at enhancing individual and collective effectiveness.

Personality encompasses the unique and enduring patterns of thoughts, feelings, and behaviours that distinguish individuals. It is shaped by a combination of genetic predispositions, environmental influences, and developmental experiences. By exploring the components of personality, theories that explain its development, and its significance in everyday life, we gain insight into what makes each person distinctive and how these characteristics influence their interactions with the world. Understanding personality is not only a cornerstone of psychology but also essential for fostering personal growth, improving interpersonal relationships, and promoting overall well-being.

Personality according to Various Spiritual Texts

Personality, as viewed through the lens of various spiritual texts and traditions, often emphasizes the deeper aspects of human nature, the development of virtues, and the attainment of spiritual maturity. While interpretations may vary across different spiritual traditions, there are common themes that highlight the essence of personality from a spiritual perspective:

Virtues and Character Development

Many spiritual traditions emphasise the cultivation of virtues and moral qualities as central to developing a positive personality:

- Christianity: The Bible encourages followers to cultivate virtues such as love, compassion, humility, patience, and forgiveness. These virtues are seen as essential for embodying the teachings of Jesus Christ and living a life aligned with God's will.
- Islam: The Quran emphasises virtues such as sincerity, patience, generosity, and justice. Muslims are encouraged to cultivate these qualities to strengthen their character and fulfil their duties towards God and humanity.
- Buddhism: Buddhist teachings focus on developing virtues such as compassion, mindfulness, wisdom, and equanimity. These virtues are seen as essential for overcoming suffering (dukkha) and achieving spiritual liberation (nirvana).
- Hinduism: Hindu scriptures emphasise the cultivation of virtues such as truthfulness (satya), non-violence (ahimsa), self-control

(dama), and compassion (daya). These virtues are integral to achieving spiritual growth and harmony with the universe.

Self-awareness and Inner Transformation

Spiritual texts often emphasise the importance of self-awareness, introspection, and inner transformation as pathways to developing a harmonious and enlightened personality:

- Taoism: Taoist teachings emphasize the cultivation of inner harmony, spontaneity, and alignment with the natural flow of life (Tao). Self-awareness and mindfulness practices are central to achieving balance and clarity of mind.
- Sufism (Islamic Mysticism): Sufi teachings focus on the purification of the soul (nafs) through practices such as dhikr (remembrance of God), meditation, and spiritual retreats (*khalwa*). This inner purification is believed to lead to spiritual enlightenment and the embodiment of divine qualities.
- Yoga Philosophy (Hinduism): In Hindu philosophy, particularly in the Yoga Sutras of Patanjali, personality development is linked to the purification of the mind (*chitta*) and the attainment of self-realisation (*atman*). Practices such as yoga (union of body, mind, and spirit), meditation (*dhyana*), and ethical living (*yamas and niyamas*) are essential for spiritual evolution.

Transcendence of Ego and Selflessness

Spiritual traditions often advocate for transcending ego-centric desires and cultivating selflessness as a means to attain spiritual maturity and realise higher states of consciousness:

- Christian Mysticism: Christian mystics emphasise the importance of self-emptying (kenosis) and surrendering to God's will. By transcending the ego and practicing humility, individuals can experience union with the divine.
- Zen Buddhism: Zen teachings focus on overcoming attachment to the ego-self (*anatman*) through practices such as meditation (*zazen*), koan introspection, and direct transmission of wisdom from master to disciple. This leads to the realisation of one's true nature (Buddha nature) and freedom from suffering.
- Judaism: Jewish mysticism (*Kabbalah*) emphasises the purification of the soul (tikkun ha-nefesh) and the cultivation of virtues such as loving-kindness (*chesed*), compassion (*rachamim*), and humility

(*anavah*). These virtues are seen as pathways to spiritual growth and union with God.

Across various spiritual texts and traditions, personality development is intricately linked to moral and spiritual growth, the cultivation of virtues, self-awareness, and transcendence of ego-centric desires. By aligning one's thoughts, actions, and intentions with spiritual principles, individuals can cultivate a positive and enlightened personality that contributes to their own spiritual journey and enhances their relationships with others and the world around them.

Significance of Yogic Practices in Personality Grooming

Yogic practices play a crucial role in grooming personality by fostering holistic development that encompasses physical health, mental well-being, emotional balance, and spiritual growth. Here are key aspects highlighting the significance of yogic practices in personality grooming:

- *Physical Health and Vitality: Yogic practices, such as asanas (poses) and pranayama* (breathing exercises), promote physical fitness, flexibility, and strength. Regular practice enhances muscle tone, improves posture, and increases overall stamina and endurance. This physical vitality not only supports a healthy body but also contributes to a confident and energetic demeanour, essential for engaging fully in daily activities and achieving personal goals.
- *Stress Reduction and Emotional Balance:* One of the profound benefits of yoga is its ability to reduce stress and promote emotional resilience. Techniques like deep breathing exercises, meditation, and mindfulness practices calm the nervous system, lower cortisol levels, and enhance emotional regulation. As individuals learn to manage stress effectively through yoga, they cultivate inner peace, mental clarity, and emotional stability. This equips them to handle challenges with composure, maintain positive relationships, and navigate life's ups and downs more gracefully.
- *Mental Clarity and Focus:* Yoga practices emphasize concentration and mindfulness, which improve cognitive function and mental clarity. Techniques such as focused breathing (*pranayama*) and meditation sharpen attention and enhance mental focus. This heightened awareness enables individuals to make decisions more thoughtfully, problem-solve effectively, and stay present in each moment. As a result, they become more productive, efficient, and

capable of achieving personal and professional goals with clarity and purpose.

- *Cultivation of Self-discipline and Self-awareness:* Yoga encourages self-discipline through regular practice and adherence to ethical principles (*yamas and niyamas*). As individuals commit to a consistent yoga routine, they cultivate self-discipline, resilience, and a sense of personal responsibility. Moreover, yoga promotes self-awareness by encouraging introspection and mindfulness of thoughts, emotions, and actions. This self-awareness fosters personal growth, facilitates positive behavioural changes, and enhances interpersonal relationships by fostering empathy and understanding.
- *Spiritual Growth and Inner Transformation:* Beyond physical and mental benefits, yogic practices facilitate spiritual growth and inner transformation. Through practices such as meditation, chanting (*mantra*), and deep relaxation (*Yoga Nidra*), individuals connect with their inner selves and explore deeper aspects of consciousness. This spiritual journey fosters a sense of purpose, inner peace, and harmony with oneself and the universe. It encourages individuals to live authentically, aligned with their values and beliefs, and to cultivate qualities such as compassion, gratitude, and humility.
- *Overall Well-being and Quality of Life:* The holistic approach of yoga integrates physical, mental, emotional, and spiritual dimensions of well-being. By nurturing all aspects of the self, yoga promotes overall wellness and enhances the quality of life. Individuals who practice yoga regularly report improved sleep, boosted immune function, reduced chronic pain, and enhanced overall vitality. This comprehensive well-being contributes to a positive outlook on life, greater resilience in facing challenges, and a balanced approach to personal and professional relationships.

Yogic practices play a transformative role in personality grooming by promoting physical health, emotional balance, mental clarity, self-discipline, spiritual growth, and overall well-being. Through the integration of yoga into daily life, individuals cultivate a harmonious and resilient personality that enhances their capacity for self-expression, meaningful relationships, and fulfilling life experiences. The profound benefits of yoga extend beyond the physical realm, empowering individuals to thrive holistically and embody their fullest potential in every aspect of life.

12

Yogic Management of Psychological Disorders

Psychological disorders, also known as mental disorders or psychiatric disorders, refer to a wide range of conditions that affect an individual's thoughts, emotions, behaviour, and overall functioning. These disorders are characterised by significant distress or impairment in social, occupational, or other important areas of life. Psychological disorders can vary widely in terms of severity, duration, and symptoms, and they often require professional diagnosis and treatment.

Types and Categories

Psychological disorders encompass a broad spectrum of conditions, including but not limited to:

Mood Disorders

- *Depressive Disorders:* Such as major depressive disorder and dysthymia, characterised by persistent feelings of sadness, hopelessness, and loss of interest in activities.
- *Bipolar Disorders:* Involving episodes of mania (elevated mood, increased energy) and depression, alternating with periods of normal mood.

Anxiety Disorders

- *Generalised Anxiety Disorder (GAD):* Excessive worry and anxiety about a variety of everyday problems.
- *Panic Disorder:* Recurrent panic attacks characterised by sudden, intense fear and physical symptoms like rapid heartbeat and sweating.
- *Phobias:* Intense fear or avoidance of specific objects or situations, such as heights (acrophobia) or spiders (arachnophobia).

Psychotic Disorders

- *Schizophrenia:* Characterised by hallucinations (perceiving things that aren't real) and delusions (false beliefs).
- *Schizoaffective Disorder:* Combines symptoms of schizophrenia with mood disorder symptoms (depression or mania).

Trauma and Stressor-Related Disorders

- *Post-Traumatic Stress Disorder (PTSD):* Occurs after experiencing or witnessing a traumatic event, leading to flashbacks, nightmares, and severe anxiety.
- *Acute Stress Disorder:* Similar symptoms to PTSD but typically occurs immediately following a traumatic event.

Personality Disorders

- *Borderline Personality Disorder:* Marked by instability in relationships, self-image, and emotions, often leading to impulsive behaviour and intense fear of abandonment.
- *Antisocial Personality Disorder:* Characterised by disregard for others' rights, deceitfulness, impulsivity, and lack of remorse.

Neurodevelopmental Disorders

- *Autism Spectrum Disorder (ASD):* Affects social interaction, communication skills, and behaviour patterns.
- *Attention-Deficit Hyperactivity Disorder (ADHD):* Involves difficulty sustaining attention, hyperactivity, and impulsivity.

Substance-related and Addictive Disorders

- *Substance Use Disorders:* Dependence on or abuse of substances such as alcohol, drugs, or medications, leading to significant impairment or distress.

Causes and Risk Factors

Psychological disorders arise from a complex interplay of genetic, biological, environmental, and psychological factors:

- *Genetic Factors:* Some disorders, such as schizophrenia and bipolar disorder, tend to run in families, suggesting a genetic predisposition.
- *Biological Factors:* Imbalances in neurotransmitters (brain chemicals) and structural abnormalities in the brain can contribute to certain disorders.
- *Environmental Factors:* Stressful life events, trauma, abuse, and significant life changes can trigger or exacerbate psychological disorders.
- *Psychological Factors:* Personality traits, coping styles, and learned patterns of behaviour can influence vulnerability to developing disorders.

Diagnosis and Treatment

Diagnosis of psychological disorders typically involves a comprehensive assessment by a mental health professional, such as a psychiatrist, psychologist, or clinical social worker. This assessment may include interviews, psychological testing, and observation of symptoms over time. Treatment approaches vary depending on the disorder and may include:

- *Psychotherapy:* Cognitive-behavioural therapy (CBT), psychodynamic therapy, and other therapeutic approaches help individuals manage symptoms, improve coping skills, and address underlying issues.
- *Medication:* Psychiatric medications, such as antidepressants, mood stabilisers, antipsychotics, and anti-anxiety medications, may be prescribed to alleviate symptoms.
- *Supportive Services:* Support groups, case management, and vocational rehabilitation programs help individuals manage daily challenges and improve overall quality of life.

Psychological disorders encompass a diverse range of conditions that affect mental health and well-being. They can significantly impact an individual's ability to function effectively in various areas of life. Understanding the causes, symptoms, and treatment options for these disorders is crucial for promoting early intervention, recovery, and improved quality of life for individuals affected by mental health challenges. Professional diagnosis and appropriate treatment, often tailored to the specific needs of each individual, play a key role in managing psychological disorders effectively.

Yogic Management of Mood Disorders

Yogic practices can be highly beneficial in managing mood disorders by promoting emotional balance, reducing stress, and enhancing overall well-being. Here are some specific yogic practices that can help individuals cope with mood disorders such as depression and anxiety:

Asanas (Yoga Poses)

- *Surya Namaskar* (Sun Salutation): This dynamic sequence of poses stretches and strengthens the entire body, increases circulation, and promotes a sense of vitality and well-being.
- *Viparita Karani* (Legs-Up-the-Wall Pose): Helps in relaxation and stress reduction by promoting blood circulation to the brain and calming the nervous system.

- *Balasana* (Child's Pose): Provides a gentle stretch for the back and helps in calming the mind and reducing anxiety.
- *Setu Bandhasana* (Bridge Pose): Opens the chest and heart area, promotes relaxation, and can help alleviate symptoms of mild depression.
- *Bhujangasana* (Cobra Pose) and *Dhanurasana* (Bow Pose): These backbends help in energising the body and improving mood by increasing circulation and releasing tension.

Pranayama (Breathing Exercises)

- *Nadi Shodhana* (Alternate Nostril Breathing): Balances the left and right hemispheres of the brain, calms the mind, and reduces stress and anxiety.
- *Bhramari Pranayama* (Humming Bee Breath): Helps in relieving tension, anxiety, and anger by promoting relaxation and soothing the nervous system.
- *Kapalabhati* (Skull-Shining Breath): Cleanses the mind and body, increases oxygen supply to the brain, and energizes the body, improving overall mood.

Meditation and Mindfulness Practices

- *Mindfulness Meditation:* Cultivates present-moment awareness, reduces rumination (repetitive negative thinking), and promotes acceptance and self-compassion.
- *Loving-Kindness Meditation* (*Metta Bhavana*): Cultivates feelings of love, compassion, and goodwill towards oneself and others, which can counteract feelings of depression and isolation.
- *Yoga Nidra* (Yogic Sleep): Deep relaxation technique that promotes restorative sleep, reduces stress, and helps in managing symptoms of anxiety and depression.

Yoga Philosophy and Lifestyle

- *Yamas and Niyamas:* Ethical principles and personal disciplines in yoga philosophy (such as non-violence, truthfulness, contentment, self-discipline) guide individuals towards a balanced and harmonious life.
- *Satvic Diet:* A balanced diet that includes fresh fruits, vegetables, whole grains, and minimal processed foods supports mental clarity and emotional stability.
- *Regular Practice:* Consistency in yoga practice, even for short durations, can have cumulative benefits in managing mood disorders by promoting routine, discipline, and self-care.

Guided Relaxation and Yoga Therapy

- *Yoga Therapy Sessions:* Tailored yoga practices under the guidance of a certified yoga therapist can address specific symptoms and challenges associated with mood disorders.
- *Guided Relaxation Techniques:* Yoga nidra, progressive muscle relaxation, and guided imagery sessions can help in reducing physical tension, calming the mind, and improving sleep quality.

Incorporating Yogic Practices for Mood Disorders

Individuals with mood disorders can benefit from incorporating yogic practices into their daily routine. Starting with a gentle practice and gradually increasing intensity and duration can help establish a sustainable routine. It's important to practice under the guidance of a qualified yoga instructor, especially when dealing with severe symptoms or specific health concerns. Yoga complements traditional treatment approaches and can provide valuable tools for managing symptoms, promoting emotional resilience, and supporting overall mental health and well-being.

Yogic Management of Anxiety Disorders

Yogic practices offer effective tools for managing anxiety disorders by promoting relaxation, calming the mind, and restoring balance to the nervous system. Here are specific practices and procedures that can help individuals cope with anxiety:

Pranayama (Breathing Exercises)

- *Diaphragmatic Breathing (Yogic Belly Breathing):* Focuses on deep, slow breaths that engage the diaphragm, promoting relaxation and calming the nervous system.
- *Sheetali and Sheetkari Pranayama*: Cooling breath techniques that involve inhaling through the mouth or curled tongue (*Sheetali*) or through the teeth (*Sheetkari*), which can help in reducing stress and anxiety.
- *Bhramari Pranayama* (Humming Bee Breath): Involves inhaling deeply and producing a humming sound during exhalation, which helps in calming the mind and reducing anxiety levels.
- *Nadi Shodhana* (Alternate Nostril Breathing): Balances the flow of energy (prana) in the body, calms the mind, and promotes mental clarity and emotional stability.

Asanas (Yoga Poses)

- *Tadasana* (Mountain Pose): Grounding pose that improves posture, enhances body awareness, and promotes a sense of stability and calm.
- *Virabhadrasana* (Warrior Pose Series): Strength-building poses that instill confidence, improve focus, and release tension in the body.
- *Uttanasana* (Standing Forward Bend): Forward bending pose that promotes relaxation, stretches the spine and hamstrings, and calms the mind.
- *Paschimottanasana* (Seated Forward Bend): Forward bending pose that stretches the entire back of the body, promotes relaxation, and relieves stress and anxiety.

Meditation and Mindfulness Practices

- *Mindfulness Meditation:* Involves focusing attention on the present moment without judgment, which helps in reducing anxiety by calming racing thoughts and promoting inner peace.
- *Body Scan Meditation:* Involves systematically focusing attention on different parts of the body, promoting relaxation and releasing physical tension associated with anxiety.
- *Loving-Kindness Meditation* (*Metta Bhavana*): Cultivates feelings of compassion and goodwill towards oneself and others, reducing self-criticism and promoting emotional resilience.

Yoga Nidra (Yogic Sleep)

- *Yoga Nidra:* Guided relaxation technique that induces deep relaxation and promotes restorative sleep, helping in reducing anxiety symptoms and improving overall well-being.

Yoga Philosophy and Lifestyle

- *Satvic Diet:* A balanced diet that includes fresh fruits, vegetables, whole grains, and minimally processed foods supports mental clarity and emotional stability, reducing anxiety triggers.
- *Daily Routine:* Establishing a consistent yoga practice routine helps in maintaining stability, discipline, and a sense of control, which are beneficial in managing anxiety.

Guided Relaxation and Yoga Therapy

- *Yoga Therapy Sessions:* Tailored yoga practices under the guidance of a certified yoga therapist can address specific symptoms and triggers associated with anxiety disorders.

- *Progressive Muscle Relaxation:* Involves tensing and relaxing muscle groups systematically, promoting physical relaxation and reducing anxiety symptoms.

Incorporating Yogic Practices for Anxiety Disorder

To effectively manage anxiety disorders, individuals can incorporate these yogic practices into their daily routine. Starting with a gentle practice and gradually increasing intensity and duration can help establish a sustainable routine. It's important to practice under the guidance of a qualified yoga instructor or therapist, especially when dealing with severe symptoms or specific health concerns. Yoga serves as a complementary approach to traditional treatments for anxiety disorders, offering valuable tools for promoting relaxation, reducing stress, and fostering emotional resilience and well-being.

Yogic Management of Psychotic Disorder

Yogic practices can provide supportive tools for managing psychotic disorders by promoting calmness, improving concentration, and fostering overall well-being. It's crucial to note that individuals with psychotic disorders should practice under the guidance of qualified professionals and in conjunction with conventional medical treatment. Here are specific practices and procedures that can be beneficial:

Pranayama (Breathing Exercises)

- *Dirga Swasam Pranayama* (Three-Part Breath): Involves deep inhalation into the abdomen, chest, and upper lungs, followed by slow exhalation, promoting relaxation and calming the mind.
- *Bhramari Pranayama* (Humming Bee Breath): Involves deep inhalation followed by making a humming sound during exhalation, which can help in reducing anxiety and promoting mental clarity.
- *Nadi Shodhana* (Alternate Nostril Breathing): Balances the flow of energy (prana) in the body, calms the mind, and enhances mental focus and stability.

Asanas (Yoga Poses)

- *Sukhasana* (Easy Pose): Cross-legged seated position that promotes grounding, relaxation, and concentration.
- *Vajrasana* (Thunderbolt Pose): Kneeling posture that enhances digestion, calms the mind, and improves blood circulation.

- *Shavasana* (Corpse Pose): Relaxation pose that promotes deep relaxation, reduces stress, and fosters overall calmness and well-being.

Meditation and Mindfulness Practices

- *Guided Visualisation:* Involves imagining peaceful and calming scenes or experiences, promoting relaxation and reducing stress and anxiety.
- *Mindfulness Meditation:* Focuses on being present in the moment without judgment, helping to cultivate inner peace and emotional stability.
- *Walking Meditation:* Mindful walking practice that promotes relaxation, grounding, and mental clarity.

Yoga Nidra (Yogic Sleep)

- *Yoga Nidra*: Guided relaxation technique that induces deep relaxation and promotes restorative sleep, helping in reducing stress and promoting overall well-being.

Yoga Philosophy and Lifestyle

- *Satvic Diet:* A balanced diet that includes fresh fruits, vegetables, whole grains, and minimally processed foods supports mental clarity and emotional stability.
- *Regular Routine:* Establishing a consistent yoga practice routine helps in maintaining stability, discipline, and a sense of control, which can be beneficial in managing symptoms of psychotic disorders.

Guided Relaxation and Yoga Therapy

- *Yoga Therapy Sessions:* Tailored yoga practices under the guidance of a certified yoga therapist can address specific symptoms and challenges associated with psychotic disorders.
- *Progressive Muscle Relaxation:* Involves tensing and relaxing muscle groups systematically, promoting physical relaxation and reducing stress.

Incorporating Yogic Practices for Psychotic Disorder

Individuals with psychotic disorders can benefit from integrating yogic practices into their daily routine, under the supervision and guidance of mental health professionals. It's essential to adapt thses practices to individual needs and capabilities, ensuring they complement medical treatment and support overall well-being. Yoga serves as a complementary approach to conventional treatments for psychotic disorders, providing valuable tools for managing symptoms, promoting relaxation, and fostering emotional resilience and stability.

Yogic Management of Trauma and Stressor-related Disorders

Yogic practices offer effective tools for managing trauma and stress-related disorders by promoting relaxation, grounding, and emotional resilience. These practices can complement conventional therapies and support individuals in coping with symptoms. Here are specific practices and procedures that can be beneficial:

Pranayama (Breathing Exercises)

- *Diaphragmatic Breathing (Yogic Belly Breathing):* Focuses on deep, slow breaths that engage the diaphragm, promoting relaxation and calming the nervous system.
- *Kapalabhati Pranayama (Skull-Shining Breath):* Involves rapid, forceful exhalations followed by passive inhalations, which helps in releasing tension and increasing mental clarity.
- *Bhramari Pranayama (Humming Bee Breath):* Involves deep inhalation followed by making a humming sound during exhalation, promoting relaxation and reducing anxiety.

Asanas (Yoga Poses)

- *Balasana* (Child's Pose): Restorative pose that promotes relaxation, stretches the spine, and releases tension in the back and shoulders.
- *Supta Baddha Konasana* (Reclining Bound Angle Pose): Opens the chest and promotes relaxation by releasing tension in the hips and groin area.
- *Setu Bandhasana* (Bridge Pose): Backbend that opens the heart center, stretches the spine, and promotes relaxation and emotional balance.

Meditation and Mindfulness Practices

- *Mindfulness Meditation:* Focuses on being present in the moment without judgment, helping to reduce stress and promote emotional resilience.
- *Body Scan Meditation:* Involves systematically scanning the body for tension and releasing it, promoting relaxation and reducing physical symptoms of stress.

- *Loving-Kindness Meditation (Metta Bhavana):* Cultivates feelings of compassion and goodwill towards oneself and others, reducing self-criticism and promoting emotional healing.

Yoga Nidra (Yogic Sleep)

- *Yoga Nidra:* Guided relaxation technique that induces deep relaxation and promotes restorative sleep, helping in reducing stress and promoting overall well-being.

Yoga Philosophy and Lifestyle

- *Satvic Diet:* A balanced diet that includes fresh fruits, vegetables, whole grains, and minimally processed foods supports mental clarity and emotional stability.
- *Routine and Structure:* Establishing a consistent yoga practice routine helps in maintaining stability, discipline, and a sense of control, which can be beneficial in managing symptoms of trauma and stress-related disorders.

Guided Relaxation and Yoga Therapy

- *Yoga Therapy Sessions:* Tailored yoga practices under the guidance of a certified yoga therapist can address specific symptoms and challenges associated with trauma and stress-related disorders.
- *Progressive Muscle Relaxation:* Involves tensing and relaxing muscle groups systematically, promoting physical relaxation and reducing symptoms of tension and stress.

Incorporating Yogic Practices for Trauma and Stressor-related Disorders

Individuals with trauma and stress-related disorders can benefit from integrating yogic practices into their daily routine, under the supervision and guidance of mental health professionals. It's essential to adapt these practices to individual needs and capabilities, ensuring they complement medical treatment and support overall well-being. Yoga serves as a complementary approach to conventional therapies for trauma and stress-related disorders, providing valuable tools for managing symptoms, promoting relaxation, and fostering emotional resilience and healing.

Yogic Management of Personality Disorders

Yogic practices can offer supportive tools for managing personality disorders by promoting self-awareness, emotional regulation, and overall well-being. These practices can complement traditional therapies and support individuals in coping with symptoms. Here are specific practices and procedures that can be beneficial:

Pranayama (Breathing Exercises)

- *Anulom Vilom Pranayama* (Alternate Nostril Breathing): Balances the flow of energy (prana) in the body, calms the mind, and enhances mental clarity and emotional stability.
- *Bhramari Pranayama* (Humming Bee Breath): Involves deep inhalation followed by making a humming sound during exhalation, promoting relaxation and reducing anxiety.
- *Sheetali Pranayama* (Cooling Breath): Involves inhaling through the curled tongue or mouth and exhaling through the nose, which cools the body and calms the mind.

Asanas (Yoga Poses)

- *Trikonasana* (Triangle Pose): Enhances balance, stability, and concentration while stretching the spine and legs, promoting physical and mental harmony.
- *Virabhadrasana* (Warrior Pose Series): Strength-building poses that instil confidence, improve focus, and release tension in the body.
- *Baddha Konasana* (Bound Angle Pose): Opens the hips and groin, promotes relaxation, and helps in reducing emotional tension and stress.

Meditation and Mindfulness Practices

- *Mindfulness Meditation:* Focuses on present-moment awareness without judgment, helping to improve self-awareness and emotional regulation.
- *Loving-Kindness Meditation* (Metta Bhavana): Cultivates feelings of compassion and goodwill towards oneself and others, reducing interpersonal conflicts and promoting emotional healing.
- *Visualisation Techniques:* Involves imagining positive outcomes and scenarios, promoting a sense of control and reducing anxiety and distress.

Yoga Nidra (Yogic Sleep)

- *Yoga Nidra:* Guided relaxation technique that induces deep relaxation and promotes restorative sleep, helping in reducing stress and promoting overall well-being.

Yoga Philosophy and Lifestyle

- *Satvic Diet:* A balanced diet that includes fresh fruits, vegetables, whole grains, and minimally processed foods supports mental clarity and emotional stability.
- *Daily Routine:* Establishing a consistent yoga practice routine helps in maintaining stability, discipline, and a sense of control, which can be beneficial in managing symptoms of personality disorders.

Guided Relaxation and Yoga Therapy

- *Yoga Therapy Sessions:* Tailored yoga practices under the guidance of a certified yoga therapist can address specific symptoms and challenges associated with personality disorders.
- *Progressive Muscle Relaxation:* Involves tensing and relaxing muscle groups systematically, promoting physical relaxation and reducing symptoms of tension and stress.

Incorporating Yogic Practices for Personality Disorders

Individuals with personality disorders can benefit from integrating these yogic practices into their daily routine, under the supervision and guidance of mental health professionals. It's essential to adapt practices to individual needs and capabilities, ensuring they complement medical treatment and support overall well-being. Yoga serves as a complementary approach to traditional therapies for personality disorders, providing valuable tools for managing symptoms, promoting self-awareness, and fostering emotional resilience and well-being.

Yogic Management of Neurodevelopmental Disorders

Yogic practices can offer supportive tools for managing neurodevelopmental disorders by promoting focus, emotional regulation, and overall well-being. These practices can complement traditional therapies and support individuals in coping with symptoms. Here are specific practices and procedures that can be beneficial:

***Pranayama* (Breathing Exercises)**

- *Bhramari Pranayama* (Humming Bee Breath): Involves deep inhalation followed by making a humming sound during exhalation, promoting relaxation and reducing anxiety.
- *Nadi Shodhana* (Alternate Nostril Breathing): Balances the flow of energy (prana) in the body, calms the mind, and enhances mental focus and stability.

- *Ujjayi Pranayama* (Victorious Breath): Involves breathing deeply through the nose with a slight constriction of the throat, promoting relaxation and concentration.

***Asanas* (Yoga Poses)**

- *Tadasana* (Mountain Pose): Promotes grounding, improves posture, and enhances body awareness and concentration.
- *Vrikshasana* (Tree Pose): Enhances balance, stability, and focus while calming the mind and improving concentration.
- *Balasana* (Child's Pose): Restorative pose that promotes relaxation, stretches the spine, and calms the nervous system.

Meditation and Mindfulness Practices

- *Mindfulness Meditation:* Focuses on present-moment awareness without judgment, helping to improve attention span and emotional regulation.
- *Visualisation Techniques:* Involves imagining positive outcomes and scenarios, promoting cognitive function and reducing stress and anxiety.
- *Yoga Nidra* (Yogic Sleep): Guided relaxation technique that induces deep relaxation and promotes restorative sleep, supporting overall well-being.

Yoga Philosophy and Lifestyle

- *Satvic-Diet:* A balanced diet that includes fresh fruits, vegetables, whole grains, and minimally processed foods supports mental clarity and emotional stability.
- *Routine and Structure:* Establishing a consistent yoga practice routine helps in maintaining stability, discipline, and a sense of control, which can be beneficial in managing symptoms of neurodevelopmental disorders.

Guided Relaxation and Yoga Therapy

- *Yoga Therapy Sessions:* Tailored yoga practices under the guidance of a certified yoga therapist can address specific symptoms and challenges associated with neurodevelopmental disorders.
- *Progressive Muscle Relaxation:* Involves tensing and relaxing muscle groups systematically, promoting physical relaxation and reducing symptoms of tension and stress.

Yogic Practices for Neurodevelopmental Disorders

Individuals with neurodevelopmental disorders can benefit from integrating yogic practices into their daily routine, under the supervision and guidance of mental health professionals. It's essential to adapt these practices to individual needs and capabilities, ensuring they complement medical treatment and support overall well-being. Yoga serves as a complementary approach to traditional therapies for neurodevelopmental disorders, providing valuable tools for managing symptoms, promoting focus, and fostering emotional resilience and well-being.

Yogic Management of Substance-related and Addictive Disorders

Yogic practices can be beneficial in supporting individuals with substance-related and addictive disorders by promoting self-awareness, reducing cravings, and fostering overall well-being. These practices can complement conventional therapies and support recovery efforts. Here are some aspects of yogic management for substance-related and addictive disorders:

Pranayama (Breathing Exercises)

- *Deep Breathing Exercises:* Techniques like Diaphragmatic Breathing (Yogic Belly Breathing) help in calming the mind, reducing anxiety, and managing cravings.
- *Kapalabhati Pranayama* (Skull-Shining Breath): Cleanses the mind and body, increases oxygen supply, and promotes mental clarity, which can aid in overcoming addictive urges.
- *Bhramari Pranayama* (Humming Bee Breath): Promotes relaxation, reduces stress, and can help manage emotional triggers associated with addiction.

Asanas (Yoga Poses)

- *Balasana* (Child's Pose): Provides relaxation, calms the nervous system, and helps in reducing stress and anxiety.
- *Surya Namaskar* (Sun Salutation): A dynamic sequence that enhances circulation, detoxifies the body, and promotes physical and mental well-being.
- *Viparita Karani* (Legs-Up-the-Wall Pose): Promotes relaxation, improves circulation, and reduces fatigue and restlessness.

Meditation and Mindfulness Practices

- *Mindfulness Meditation:* Cultivates awareness of thoughts and emotions without judgment, aiding in recognising triggers and developing healthier responses.
- *Yoga Nidra* (Yogic Sleep): Deep relaxation technique that reduces stress, enhances self-awareness, and supports recovery by promoting restorative sleep.

- *Loving-Kindness Meditation (Metta Bhavana):* Fosters compassion towards oneself and others, promoting emotional resilience and reducing self-criticism.

Yoga Philosophy and Lifestyle

- *Satvic Diet:* Emphasises fresh fruits, vegetables, whole grains, and hydrating fluids, supporting detoxification and overall well-being.
- *Routine and Structure:* Establishing a consistent yoga practice routine provides stability, discipline, and a positive outlet, reducing the likelihood of relapse.

Guided Relaxation and Yoga Therapy

- *Yoga Therapy Sessions:* Tailored practices under the guidance of a certified yoga therapist address specific challenges and support recovery goals.
- *Group Yoga Classes:* Offer social support, promote a sense of community, and provide a healthy alternative to addictive behaviours.

Integrating yogic practices into daily life can enhance overall well-being and support recovery from substance-related and addictive disorders. It's essential for individuals to practice under the guidance of qualified instructors or therapists, ensuring practices are safe and effective for their specific needs. Yoga serves as a holistic approach to recovery, addressing physical, mental, and emotional aspects while promoting long-term health and wellness.

Yoga has a profound effect on psychological well-being, playing a vital role in enhancing mental health through various mechanisms. The practice of yoga involves a combination of physical postures (*asanas*), breathing exercises (*pranayama*), and meditation, which together contribute to reducing stress, anxiety, and depression. *Asanas* improve blood circulation and stimulate the release of endorphins, the body's natural mood lifters, promoting a sense of well-being and relaxation. *Pranayama*, or breath control, helps in regulating the autonomic nervous system, reducing the stress response, and promoting a state of calm and mental clarity. These practices lead to the reduction of cortisol levels, the primary stress hormone, thereby alleviating symptoms of anxiety and depression and enhancing overall emotional stability.

Furthermore, yoga fosters mindfulness and self-awareness, which are crucial for psychological resilience. Meditation practices included in yoga enhance the brain's ability to focus and remain present, reducing the impact of intrusive thoughts and promoting a positive outlook. Regular yoga practice increases the production of gamma-aminobutyric acid (GABA), a neurotransmitter associated with improved mood and reduced anxiety. It also enhances neuroplasticity, the brain's ability to adapt and reorganize itself, which is beneficial for cognitive functions and emotional regulation. By integrating mind and body, yoga helps individuals develop a balanced state of being, promoting emotional intelligence, self-compassion, and a deeper connection to oneself and others. This holistic approach to mental health makes yoga a powerful tool for psychological well-being and personal growth.

13

Yoga for Neurological Disorders

Yoga, an ancient practice rooted in Indian philosophy, has gained widespread recognition for its holistic health benefits, particularly in the management of neurological disorders. Neurological disorders encompass a wide range of conditions affecting the nervous system, including multiple sclerosis, epilepsy, Parkinson's disease, and stroke. These conditions often lead to significant physical, cognitive, and emotional challenges, impacting the quality of life. Integrating yoga into the treatment and management plan for neurological disorders can offer a complementary approach that enhances conventional medical treatments. Through a combination of physical postures, breathing exercises, and meditation, yoga provides a multi-faceted approach to improving neurological health and overall well-being.

One of the primary ways yoga benefits individuals with neurological disorders is by promoting neuroplasticity—the brain's ability to adapt and reorganise itself. Regular practice of yoga has been shown to enhance brain function, improve motor skills, and increase cognitive flexibility. The physical postures, or *asanas*, help in maintaining muscle strength and coordination, which can be particularly beneficial for conditions like Parkinson's disease and multiple sclerosis, where motor control is compromised. Additionally, the breathing exercises and meditation components of yoga play a crucial role in reducing stress and anxiety, which are common comorbidities in neurological disorders. By fostering a sense of calm and relaxation, yoga helps in regulating the autonomic nervous system, reducing the frequency and severity of neurological symptoms. This integrative approach not only supports physical health but also promotes mental and emotional resilience, making yoga a valuable tool in the comprehensive management of neurological disorders.

Modern Epidemic: Challenges in the Context of Neurological Disorders

The modern era, characterised by rapid technological advancements, urbanisation, and lifestyle changes, has brought about significant improvements in various aspects of human life. However, it has also introduced new challenges, particularly concerning neurological health. Neurological disorders, which encompass a wide range of conditions affecting the nervous system, have become increasingly prevalent. Conditions such as Alzheimer's disease, Parkinson's disease, epilepsy, multiple sclerosis, and stroke are not only more common but also present unique challenges in the modern context. This unit explores the myriad problems individuals face due to neurological disorders in today's fast-paced world.

Neurological Disorders Faced

Rising Prevalence and Diagnostic Challenges

One of the most pressing issues is the rising prevalence of neurological disorders. Factors such as an aging population, increased life expectancy, and better diagnostic tools have led to a higher detection rate of these conditions. However, early diagnosis remains a challenge. Many neurological disorders, such as Alzheimer's and Parkinson's, have insidious onset and are often diagnosed at advanced stages when treatment options are limited. This delay in diagnosis can significantly affect the quality of life and prognosis for individuals.

Lifestyle and Environmental Factors

Modern lifestyles contribute significantly to the onset and progression of neurological disorders. Sedentary behaviours, poor dietary habits, high-stress levels, and inadequate sleep are all factors that negatively impact neurological health. Urbanisation has led to increased exposure to pollutants and toxins, which have been linked to various neurological conditions. Additionally, the pervasive use of digital devices and the internet can lead to screen addiction and disrupt sleep patterns, further exacerbating neurological issues.

Economic and Social Burden

The economic and social burden of neurological disorders is immense. The cost of medical care, including frequent doctor visits, medications, and long-term care, can be overwhelming for individuals and their families. Many neurological disorders require lifelong management, which places a significant financial strain on healthcare systems and social support networks. Furthermore, individuals with these conditions often face social isolation and stigma, which can lead to depression and anxiety, compounding their health problems.

Access to Healthcare and Treatment Disparities

Access to healthcare and treatment for neurological disorders varies widely. In many regions, especially in low- and middle-income countries, there is a lack of specialised healthcare professionals and facilities to diagnose and treat these conditions effectively. Even in developed countries, there are disparities in access to care based on socioeconomic status, geographic location, and race. This inequity leads to delayed diagnoses, suboptimal treatment, and poorer health outcomes for many individuals.

Psychological Impact

The psychological impact of living with a neurological disorder can be profound. Chronic pain, mobility issues, cognitive decline, and the unpredictability of symptoms can lead to significant mental health challenges. Anxiety, depression, and other mood disorders are common among individuals with neurological conditions, further affecting their quality of life and ability to manage their condition. The emotional toll on caregivers is also considerable, as they often experience stress, burnout, and a sense of helplessness.

Technological and Therapeutic Advancements

Despite these challenges, there have been significant advancements in the diagnosis and treatment of neurological disorders. Innovations in neuroimaging, genetic research, and neuropharmacology have improved our understanding of these conditions and led to the development of new treatments. However, the integration of these advancements into standard clinical practice remains uneven, and many patients do not have access to the latest therapies and technologies.

Neurological disorders in the modern era present a complex set of challenges that affect individuals, families, and society at large. While advancements in medical science offer hope, there is a pressing need for comprehensive strategies that address the multifaceted nature of these conditions. This includes promoting healthy lifestyles, improving early diagnosis, ensuring equitable access to care, and providing robust support systems for individuals and caregivers. By addressing these challenges, we can improve the quality of life for those affected by neurological disorders and reduce their overall burden on society.

Yoga as a Remedy for Neurological Disorders: A Holistic Approach

In the context of the modern era's neurological health challenges, yoga has emerged as a promising complementary therapy that offers a holistic approach to managing and potentially mitigating the effects of neurological disorders. With its roots in ancient Indian philosophy, yoga integrates physical postures (*asanas*), breathing exercises (*pranayama*), and meditation, all of which collectively contribute to improving physical, mental, and emotional well-being. This section explores how yoga can serve as a key remedy for overcoming the complexities of neurological disorders.

Enhancing Neuroplasticity and Cognitive Function

One of the most significant benefits of yoga in managing neurological disorders is its ability to enhance neuroplasticity—the brain's capacity to reorganise itself by forming new neural connections. Regular practice of yoga has been shown to stimulate the brain, improve cognitive functions, and increase neuroplasticity. For individuals with conditions such as Alzheimer's disease and multiple sclerosis, yoga can help in maintaining and improving cognitive abilities, including memory, attention, and executive functions.

Reducing Stress and Anxiety

Neurological disorders are often accompanied by high levels of stress and anxiety, which can worsen symptoms and impact overall health. Yoga's focus on breath control and mindfulness helps activate the parasympathetic nervous system, which counteracts the body's stress response. Techniques such as diaphragmatic breathing, alternate nostril breathing (Nadi Shodhana), and deep relaxation practices like Yoga Nidra significantly reduce cortisol levels, the primary stress hormone. This reduction in stress and anxiety levels can lead to improved emotional stability and a better quality of life for individuals with neurological disorders.

Improving Motor Skills and Physical Stability

For disorders that affect motor skills and coordination, such as Parkinson's disease and stroke, yoga can be particularly beneficial. *Asanas* like *Tadasana* (Mountain Pose), *Vrikshasana* (Tree Pose), and *Trikonasana* (Triangle Pose) help improve balance, flexibility, and muscle strength. These physical benefits translate into better motor control, a reduced risk of falls, and enhanced overall physical stability. The slow, deliberate movements in yoga also promote proprioception—the body's ability to sense its position in space—which is crucial for individuals with impaired motor functions.

Enhancing Emotional Resilience and Mental Health

The psychological impact of neurological disorders can be profound, often leading to conditions such as depression and chronic anxiety. Yoga fosters emotional resilience through practices that promote self-awareness and self-compassion. Meditation techniques, including mindfulness meditation and loving-kindness meditation (Metta Bhavana), encourage a positive mental outlook and help in managing negative thought patterns. This enhanced emotional resilience supports better mental health and aids in coping with the daily challenges posed by neurological disorders.

Promoting Overall Well-being and Lifestyle Changes

In addition to specific physical and psychological benefits, yoga promotes an overall sense of well-being and encourages healthy lifestyle changes. The holistic nature of yoga encompasses dietary recommendations, ethical guidelines, and daily routines that support a balanced and healthy life. A Satvic diet, which emphasises fresh fruits, vegetables, whole grains, and minimal processing, complements yoga practices by supporting physical and mental health. Adopting a structured routine that includes regular yoga practice can provide a sense of stability and control, which is particularly beneficial for individuals managing chronic conditions.

Integrating yoga into the treatment plan for neurological disorders offers a multifaceted approach that addresses the physical, mental, and emotional aspects of these conditions. While it is not a cure, yoga provides valuable tools that can enhance the quality of life, improve symptoms, and support overall well-being. As a complementary therapy, yoga aligns well with conventional treatments, making it a key remedy in the holistic management of neurological disorders. Encouraging regular practice, under the guidance of qualified instructors, can help individuals harness the full potential of yoga to navigate the complexities of neurological health in the modern era.

Specific Yoga Capsules to Prevent Neurological Diseases

Preventing neurological diseases through yoga involves a combination of specific *asanas* (postures), *pranayama* (breathing exercises), and meditation techniques that support brain health, enhance neuroplasticity, and reduce stress. Here is a comprehensive yoga capsule designed to promote neurological well-being, along with guidelines on duration and frequency.

Morning Routine (30–45 Minutes)

Asanas (30 Minutes)

Surya Namaskar (Sun Salutation)
- Practice 5–10 rounds (each round includes both sides)
- Benefits: Enhances blood circulation, promotes flexibility, and energizes the body.

Tadasana (Mountain Pose)
- Hold for 1 minute
- Benefits: Improves posture, balance, and focus.

Vrikshasana (Tree Pose)
- Hold for 1 minute on each side
- Benefits: Enhances balance, coordination, and concentration.

Trikonasana (Triangle Pose)
- Hold for 1 minute on each side
- Benefits: Stretches the spine, improves flexibility, and stimulates the nervous system.

Bhujangasana (Cobra Pose)
- Hold for 1 minute
- Benefits: Strengthens the spine, opens the chest, and promotes spinal flexibility.

Shavasana (Corpse Pose)
- Hold for 5 minutes
- Benefits: Promotes relaxation and reduces stress.

Pranayama (15 Minutes)
- *Nadi Shodhana* (Alternate Nostril Breathing)
- Practice for 5 minutes
- Benefits: Balances the nervous system and reduces stress.

Bhramari Pranayama (Humming Bee Breath)
- Practice for 5 minutes
- Benefits: Calms the mind and reduces anxiety.
- *Kapalabhati Pranayama* (Skull-Shining Breath)

- Practice for 5 minutes (30 breaths per round, 3 rounds)
- Benefits: Increases oxygen supply to the brain and improves mental clarity.

Evening Routine (30 Minutes)

***Asanas* (15 Minutes)**

Adho Mukha Svanasana (Downward Dog)

- Hold for 1 minute
- Benefits: Enhances blood flow to the brain and improves strength.

Paschimottanasana (Seated Forward Bend)

- Hold for 1–2 minutes
- Benefits: Stretches the spine and calms the mind.

Setu Bandhasana (Bridge Pose)

- Hold for 1–2 minutes
- Benefits: Strengthens the back and improves circulation to the brain.
- *Viparita Karani* (Legs-Up-the-Wall Pose)
- Hold for 5 minutes
- Benefits: Promotes relaxation and reduces stress.

***Meditation* (15 Minutes)**

- Mindfulness Meditation
- Practice for 10 minutes
- Benefits: Enhances present-moment awareness and reduces stress.
- Loving-Kindness Meditation (Metta Bhavana)
- Practice for 5 minutes
- Benefits: Fosters positive emotions and emotional resilience.

Weekly Routine (1 Hour, Once a Week)

Yoga Nidra (Yogic Sleep)

- Practice for 30–45 minutes
- Benefits: Provides deep relaxation, reduces stress, and promotes restorative sleep.

Group Yoga Session

Participate in a guided group session to promote social interaction and collective energy.

Practice Guidelines

- *Duration:* Engage in the morning routine for 30–45 minutes and the evening routine for 30 minutes daily.
- *Frequency:* Practice the weekly routine once a week.

- *Consistency:* For best results, maintain this routine consistently for at least 3 months.
- *Rounds:* Follow the specified rounds for each *pranayama* practice and *asana* hold times as detailed above.

This specific yoga capsule is designed to prevent neurological diseases by promoting brain health, reducing stress, and enhancing overall well-being. Consistent practice of these *asanas*, *pranayama*, and meditation techniques can support neurological function and contribute to long-term health. It is advisable to practice under the guidance of a certified yoga instructor, especially for beginners, to ensure correct technique and avoid injury.

14

Yoga for Addicted People and Their Rehabilitation

Addiction, whether to substances such as drugs and alcohol or behaviours like gambling, represents a significant challenge that impacts not only physical health but also mental and emotional well-being. The journey to recovery often involves addressing deep-rooted psychological issues, managing withdrawal symptoms, and rebuilding a healthy lifestyle. In this context, yoga has emerged as a powerful complementary therapy that supports the rehabilitation process. Through a combination of physical postures (*asanas*), breathing exercises (*pranayama*), and meditation, yoga provides a holistic approach that can help individuals overcome addiction and regain control of their lives.

One of the primary benefits of yoga in addiction recovery is its ability to promote emotional and mental stability. Regular practice of yoga helps to reduce stress and anxiety, which are common triggers for relapse. Techniques such as deep breathing and mindfulness meditation foster a state of calm and enhance self-awareness, enabling individuals to better manage cravings and emotional triggers. Moreover, yoga supports the detoxification process by improving blood circulation and stimulating the lymphatic system, aiding in the removal of toxins from the body. This physical detoxification, combined with the mental clarity gained from yoga practices, creates a solid foundation for sustained recovery and long-term health.

Modern Era Challenges: Addiction and Rehabilitation

In the modern era, characterised by rapid technological advancements, urbanisation, and fast-paced lifestyles, addiction has emerged as a pervasive issue affecting millions worldwide. Whether it is substance abuse, alcohol dependency, or behavioural addictions such as gambling and internet addiction, the repercussions are profound and multifaceted. The problems associated with addiction are not confined to individual suffering but extend to families, communities, and society at large. This part delves into the complexities of addiction in the contemporary world and the challenges faced in rehabilitation efforts.

Rise of Addiction in the Modern Era

The modern lifestyle has inadvertently fostered an environment where addiction can thrive. The stress and pressures associated with fast-paced living, along with the easy availability of addictive substances and activities, have contributed to an increase in addiction rates. Technological advancements, while beneficial in many ways, have also introduced new avenues for addiction, such as social media, online gaming, and pornography. These addictions can be as debilitating as substance abuse, leading to significant impairments in daily functioning and mental health.

One of the critical issues in the modern context is the normalisation and glamorisation of addictive behaviours. The media's portrayal of substance use and the pervasive culture of instant gratification can obscure the dangers associated with addiction. This societal perspective often delays recognition and acceptance of the problem, hindering timely intervention and treatment.

Barriers to Effective Rehabilitation

Rehabilitation for addiction is fraught with numerous challenges. The stigma surrounding addiction is a significant barrier that prevents many individuals from seeking the help they need. This stigma can be particularly strong in certain cultures and communities, where addiction is viewed as a moral failing rather than a medical condition. Consequently, individuals may suffer in silence, worsening their condition.

Access to quality rehabilitation services is a critical issue. While there are numerous rehabilitation centers and programmes available, the quality and comprehensiveness of these services can vary widely. In many regions, especially in low- and middle-income countries, there is a shortage of trained professionals and adequate facilities. Even in developed countries, disparities in healthcare access based on socioeconomic status, geographic location, and insurance coverage can prevent individuals from receiving the care they need.

Psychological and Emotional Toll

Addiction takes a significant psychological and emotional toll on individuals. The cycle of dependency, withdrawal, and relapse can lead to feelings of hopelessness and despair. Mental health conditions such as depression, anxiety, and post-traumatic stress disorder (PTSD) are commonly comorbid with addiction, creating a complex interplay that complicates treatment. The emotional burden is not limited to the individual; families and loved ones also experience stress, financial strain, and emotional distress.

Role of Integrated Treatment Approaches

Given the multifaceted nature of addiction, integrated treatment approaches that address the physical, psychological, and social aspects of the disorder are essential. Evidence-based therapies such as cognitive-behavioral therapy (CBT), motivational interviewing, and contingency management have shown efficacy in treating addiction. However, these approaches must be tailored to the individual's unique needs and circumstances.

Complementary therapies such as yoga, mindfulness meditation, and art therapy are gaining recognition for their role in addiction rehabilitation. These practices can help individuals develop coping strategies, enhance self-awareness, and reduce stress, supporting long-term recovery. Yoga, in particular, offers a holistic approach that integrates physical health with mental and emotional well-being, making it a valuable tool in the rehabilitation process.

Policy and Community Support

Effective addiction rehabilitation requires robust policy support and community involvement. Governments and policymakers need to prioritise mental health and addiction services, ensuring adequate funding and access to quality care. Public health campaigns can play a crucial role in reducing stigma and increasing awareness about the importance of seeking help.

Community-based support systems, such as peer support groups and family therapy, are also vital in fostering a supportive environment for recovery. These networks provide individuals with a sense of belonging and accountability, which can be instrumental in preventing relapse and promoting sustained recovery.

Addiction in the modern era presents a complex challenge that requires a comprehensive and multifaceted response. Addressing the problem effectively involves overcoming stigma, improving access to quality rehabilitation services, and integrating holistic treatment approaches. By fostering a supportive environment through policy, community engagement, and innovative therapies, we can better support individuals on their journey to recovery and create a healthier society.

Yoga as a Key Remedy for Overcoming Addiction and Aiding Rehabilitation

In the modern era, addiction has become a pervasive issue, with various substances and behaviours causing significant physical, mental, and emotional harm. Overcoming addiction and achieving long-term rehabilitation is a complex process that often requires a multifaceted approach. Among the various complementary therapies available, yoga has emerged as a powerful tool in combating addiction and supporting recovery. With its combination of physical postures (*asanas*), breathing exercises (*pranayama*), and meditation, yoga offers a holistic approach that addresses the root causes of addiction, promotes healing, and supports sustained sobriety.

How Yoga Helps in Overcoming Addiction

Reducing Stress and Anxiety

- *Pranayama*: Breathing exercises such as *Nadi Shodhana* (Alternate Nostril Breathing) and *Bhramari* (Humming Bee Breath) can help calm the mind, reduce stress, and alleviate anxiety. These techniques activate the parasympathetic nervous system, which counteracts the stress response, reducing cortisol levels and promoting relaxation.
- *Meditation:* Mindfulness meditation and *Yoga Nidra* (Yogic Sleep) promote deep relaxation and help individuals cultivate a sense of inner peace. These practices can reduce the craving for addictive substances by addressing the emotional triggers that often contribute to substance use.

Improving Physical Health and Detoxification

- *Asanas*: Physical postures such as Surya Namaskar (Sun Salutation), *Bhujangasana* (Cobra Pose), and *Setu Bandhasana* (Bridge Pose) enhance blood circulation, stimulate the lymphatic system, and promote detoxification. Regular practice of these *asanas* helps in the removal of toxins from the body, supports the healing of damaged tissues, and improves overall physical health.
- *Dynamic Practices:* Incorporating dynamic sequences like Vinyasa flow can help build strength, flexibility, and endurance, which are

crucial for individuals recovering from addiction who may have experienced physical deterioration.

Enhancing Emotional Resilience and Self-Awareness

- *Mindfulness and Self-Compassion:* Yoga encourages self-awareness and self-compassion, which are essential for emotional healing. Practices like Loving-Kindness Meditation (*Metta Bhavana*) promote positive emotions and help individuals develop a compassionate attitude towards themselves and others, reducing feelings of guilt and shame often associated with addiction.
- *Emotional Regulation:* Regular yoga practice enhances the ability to regulate emotions, making it easier to manage cravings and resist the urge to relapse. Techniques like *Savasana* (Corpse Pose) and restorative yoga help in grounding emotions and providing a safe space for emotional release.

Building a Supportive Community

- *Group Classes:* Participating in group yoga classes fosters a sense of community and belonging, which can be incredibly supportive for individuals in recovery. The shared experience of practicing yoga creates a network of support and encouragement, reducing feelings of isolation.
- *Peer Support:* Engaging in yoga retreats and workshops focused on addiction recovery can provide peer support and inspiration, helping individuals stay committed to their recovery journey.

Specific Yoga Capsules for Addiction Rehabilitation

To effectively use yoga as a remedy for overcoming addiction, a structured practice routine is essential. Here is a tailored yoga capsule designed for addiction rehabilitation:

Morning Routine (45–60 Minutes)

- *Surya Namaskar* (Sun Salutation): 5–10 rounds to energise the body and mind.
- *Tadasana* (Mountain Pose): Hold for 1 minute to improve posture and focus.
- *Vrikshasana* (Tree Pose): Hold for 1 minute on each side to enhance balance and concentration.
- *Bhujangasana* (Cobra Pose): Hold for 1 minute to strengthen the spine and improve circulation.

- *Setu Bandhasana* (Bridge Pose): Hold for 1 minute to open the chest and stimulate the nervous system.
- *Shavasana* (Corpse Pose): Hold for 5 minutes to promote relaxation.

Pranayama (15 Minutes)

- *Nadi Shodhana* (Alternate Nostril Breathing): Practice for 5 minutes to balance the nervous system.
- *Bhramari Pranayama* (Humming Bee Breath): Practice for 5 minutes to calm the mind.
- *Kapalabhati Pranayama* (Skull-Shining Breath): Practice for 5 minutes (30 breaths per round, 3 rounds) to detoxify and energize the body.

Evening Routine (30 Minutes)

- *Adho Mukha Svanasana* (Downward Dog): Hold for 1 minute to enhance blood flow to the brain.
- *Paschimottanasana* (Seated Forward Bend): Hold for 1–2 minutes to stretch the spine and calm the mind.
- *Viparita Karani* (Legs-Up-the-Wall Pose): Hold for 5 minutes to promote relaxation.
- Mindfulness Meditation: Practice for 10 minutes to enhance present-moment awareness and reduce stress.

Weekly Routine (1 Hour, Once a Week)

- *Yoga Nidra* (Yogic Sleep): Practice for 30–45 minutes to provide deep relaxation and reduce stress.
- Group Yoga Session: Participate in a guided group session to promote social interaction and collective energy.

Yoga offers a comprehensive and effective approach to overcoming addiction and supporting long-term rehabilitation. By reducing stress, improving physical health, enhancing emotional resilience, and fostering a supportive community, yoga addresses the multifaceted challenges of addiction. Integrating yoga into addiction treatment plans can significantly enhance the recovery process, providing individuals with the tools they need to achieve sustained sobriety and improved overall well-being. With consistent practice and guidance from qualified instructors, yoga can be a transformative force in the journey towards recovery.

In conclusion, the integration of yogic practices into the management of addiction offers a powerful, holistic approach that addresses physical, mental, and emotional dimensions of recovery. By reducing stress and anxiety, enhancing emotional resilience, improving physical health, and fostering a supportive community, yoga provides essential tools for individuals striving to overcome addiction. The structured routines of *asanas*, pranayama, and meditation not only support detoxification and healing but also promote long-term sobriety and overall well-being. As a complementary therapy, yoga aligns seamlessly with conventional treatments, making it a vital component in the comprehensive management of addiction. With dedicated practice and professional guidance, yoga can significantly enhance the recovery journey, empowering individuals to reclaim their lives and achieve lasting transformation.

15

Yoga for Prisoner's Rehabilitation

The rehabilitation of prisoners is a critical component of the criminal justice system, aiming to reintegrate individuals into society as productive and law-abiding citizens. However, the environment within correctional facilities often poses significant challenges to mental and physical well-being. Yoga, with its holistic approach to health and wellness, has emerged as an effective tool for supporting the rehabilitation process of incarcerated individuals. By integrating physical postures (*asanas*), breathing exercises (*pranayama*), and meditation, yoga can address the complex needs of prisoners, promoting emotional stability, mental clarity, and physical health.

Yoga's impact on mental health is particularly valuable in the prison context, where inmates often experience high levels of stress, anxiety, and depression. Regular practice of yoga can help alleviate these issues by reducing stress hormones and promoting a sense of calm and inner peace. Techniques such as mindfulness meditation and deep breathing exercises foster self-awareness and emotional regulation, which are essential for managing the intense emotions and challenging situations encountered in prison life. Moreover, yoga encourages a shift towards positive thinking and self-compassion, assisting inmates in developing healthier mindsets and reducing recidivism.

In addition to its mental health benefits, yoga contributes to physical well-being, which is often compromised in the prison environment due to limited access to fitness facilities and recreational activities. Yoga *asanas* improve flexibility, strength, and overall fitness, helping inmates maintain their physical health and prevent chronic conditions associated with a sedentary lifestyle. Furthermore, the practice of yoga instills discipline and a sense of routine, which can be transformative for inmates as they prepare for reintegration into society. By fostering holistic well-being, yoga serves as a powerful rehabilitative tool that supports the journey towards rehabilitation and successful reentry into the community.

Problems that Prisoners are facing in Modern Society

Prisoners face a multitude of challenges in the modern era, reflecting the complexities of incarceration and its impact on individuals. These challenges can vary widely depending on factors such as the prison environment, socio-economic background, and the nature of their offenses. Here are some common problems prisoners often encounter:

- *Overcrowding and Living Conditions:* Prisons worldwide frequently struggle with overcrowding, leading to cramped living spaces, inadequate sanitation facilities, and increased tensions among inmates. Overcrowding can also strain resources, limiting access to healthcare, educational programmes, and recreational activities, which are essential for rehabilitation.
- *Violence and Safety Concerns:* Violence, both among inmates and involving prison staff, is a significant issue in many correctional facilities. Gang-related activities, disputes over territory or resources, and the presence of hardened criminals can contribute to an unsafe environment. The lack of effective security measures can exacerbate these issues, posing serious risks to the physical and mental well-being of prisoners.
- *Healthcare and Mental Health Services:* Access to adequate healthcare, including treatment for chronic conditions and mental health disorders, is often limited in prisons. Mental health issues such as depression, anxiety, and post-traumatic stress disorder (PTSD) are prevalent among inmates due to the stress of incarceration, isolation from family and support networks, and exposure to trauma.
- *Isolation and Lack of Social Support:* Prisoners often experience social isolation, separated from family, friends, and community support networks. This isolation can contribute to feelings of loneliness, despair, and alienation, impacting their emotional well-being and rehabilitation prospects. Maintaining connections with the outside world through visits, letters, or phone calls is crucial but can be challenging due to logistical and financial barriers.
- *Limited Rehabilitation and Educational Opportunities:* Access to educational programmes, vocational training, and rehabilitation services varies widely across prisons. Limited opportunities for skill development and reintegration programmes can hinder prisoners' ability to successfully reintegrate into society upon release. This lack of preparation can perpetuate cycles of recidivism, where individuals return to criminal behaviour due to a lack of viable alternatives.

- *Legal and Human Rights Issues:* Prisoners may face violations of their legal rights, including inadequate legal representation, prolonged pre-trial detention, and harsh sentencing practices. Human rights abuses such as solitary confinement, forced labour, and lack of access to legal recourse can further exacerbate the challenges faced by prisoners and undermine their dignity and well-being.
- *Stigma and Reintegration Challenges:* Upon release, former prisoners often encounter stigma, discrimination, and barriers to employment, housing, and social services. Reintegrating into society after incarceration can be daunting, especially for those with limited support networks or a history of substance abuse or mental health issues.

The problems faced by prisoners in the modern era are complex and multifaceted, highlighting the need for comprehensive reforms in criminal justice systems worldwide. Addressing these challenges requires a holistic approach that prioritises rehabilitation, respect for human rights, and support for reintegration into society. By recognising and addressing the systemic issues that contribute to these problems, societies can work towards creating safer, more humane, and effective correctional systems that promote justice, rehabilitation, and societal well-being.

Yoga: A Holistic Remedy for Prisoners' Rehabilitation

In the realm of prisoner rehabilitation, where challenges like overcrowding, violence, and limited resources are prevalent, yoga emerges as a transformative tool offering holistic benefits for physical, mental, and emotional well-being. Through a structured practice of physical postures (*asanas*), breathing techniques (*pranayama*), and meditation, yoga not only addresses the immediate stresses of incarceration but also supports long-term rehabilitation by fostering self-awareness, emotional resilience, and positive behavioural changes.

Physiological Benefits of Yoga for Prisoners

Stress Reduction and Relaxation

Asanas: Yoga postures such as *Savasana* (Corpse Pose), *Balasana* (Child's Pose), and *Viparita Karani* (Legs-Up-the-Wall Pose) promote relaxation by releasing tension from the body and calming the nervous system. These poses improve blood circulation, reduce cortisol levels (the stress hormone), and alleviate physical symptoms of stress commonly experienced in prison environments.

Improved Physical Health

Asanas and *Pranayama*: Regular practice of yoga enhances physical fitness by improving flexibility, strength, and cardiovascular health. Poses like *Surya Namaskar* (Sun Salutation) and Warrior Poses (*Virabhadrasana*) promote muscle tone and overall agility, which may be compromised due to limited movement and confinement in prison.

Enhanced Respiratory Function

Pranayama: Techniques such as *Dirga Pranayama* (Three-Part Breath) and Kapalabhati (Skull-Shining Breath) improve lung capacity and respiratory efficiency. These practices help prisoners develop healthier breathing patterns, reduce breathlessness, and increase oxygen supply to the brain and body, aiding in overall well-being.

Strengthened Immune System

Yoga's Mind-Body Connection: The integration of physical postures with mindful breathing enhances the body's immune response by reducing inflammation and promoting cellular regeneration. This holistic approach supports prisoners' immune systems, potentially mitigating the effects of chronic stress and improving overall health outcomes.

Pain Management and Rehabilitation

Therapeutic Benefits: Yoga therapy techniques, such as gentle stretches and relaxation exercises, help manage chronic pain conditions commonly experienced by prisoners. These practices promote healing, reduce reliance on medication for pain management, and empower individuals to take an active role in their rehabilitation journey.

Psychological and Behavioural Benefits

Beyond its physiological advantages, Yoga offers profound psychological and behavioural benefits crucial for prisoners' rehabilitation.

- *Emotional Regulation:* Yoga practices cultivate emotional resilience and self-awareness, enabling prisoners to manage anger, anxiety, and depression effectively. Techniques like mindfulness meditation and Loving-Kindness Meditation foster compassion towards oneself and others, promoting healthier interpersonal relationships.
- *Stress Management:* By reducing stress levels and promoting relaxation, yoga equips prisoners with coping mechanisms to navigate the challenges of incarceration. This resilience is essential

for maintaining mental well-being and reducing the risk of behavioural incidents within correctional facilities.

- *Positive Behaviour Reinforcement:* The discipline and structure inherent in yoga practice support positive behavioural changes among prisoners. Consistent participation in yoga sessions encourages commitment, patience, and self-discipline, qualities that are beneficial for rehabilitation and successful reintegration into society.

Yoga serves as a powerful and easily accessible solution for enhancing prisoners' rehabilitation efforts. By addressing both physiological and psychological aspects of well-being, yoga supports inmates in developing healthier lifestyles, managing stress effectively, and cultivating positive behavioural changes. As correctional facilities increasingly recognise the benefits of holistic approaches to rehabilitation, integrating yoga into rehabilitation programmes holds immense potential for transforming the lives of prisoners and fostering a more rehabilitative and humane prison environment.

Yogic Practices for Prisoners' Rehabilitation

Creating a step-by-step guide to Yogic Practices for Prisoners' rehabilitation involves tailoring practices that are accessible, safe, and beneficial within the constraints of correctional facilities. Here's a structured approach:

Step-by-Step Guide to Yogic Practices for Prisoners' Rehabilitation

Step 1: Introduction and Preparation

- *Introduce Yoga:* Begin by explaining the benefits of yoga for physical, mental, and emotional well-being. Emphasise its role in stress reduction, improving flexibility, and promoting relaxation.
- *Create a Safe Space:* Designate a quiet and clean area within the facility where prisoners can practice yoga without distractions.
- *Obtain Consent:* Ensure prisoners understand and voluntarily participate in yoga sessions. Respect individual preferences and limitations.

Step 2: Warm-up and Centreing

- *Gentle Movements:* Start with gentle warm-up exercises to loosen muscles and joints. Include simple stretches and movements to prepare the body for yoga postures.

- *Breathing Exercises (Pranayama):* Practice deep breathing techniques to calm the mind and focus attention. Begin with *Dirga Pranayama* (Three-Part Breath) or *Ujjayi Pranayama* (Victorious Breath).

Step 3: Yoga Asanas (Postures)

- *Beginner-Friendly Poses:* Choose yoga poses that are accessible and safe for all participants. Include:
  - *Tadasana* (Mountain Pose): Stand tall with feet together, arms relaxed by the sides.
  - *Vrikshasana* (Tree Pose): Stand on one leg with the other foot resting on the inner thigh or calf, hands in prayer position.
  - *Balasana* (Child's Pose): Kneel on the floor, sit back on your heels, and stretch your arms forward with forehead resting on the mat.
- *Adapt for Limited Space:* Modify poses if space is restricted, focusing on seated or standing variations that can be performed within confined areas.

Step 4: Relaxation and Meditation

- *Savasana (Corpse Pose):* Guide prisoners into a relaxation pose where they lie flat on their backs, arms by their sides, and eyes closed. Encourage deep relaxation and release of tension.
- *Mindfulness Meditation:* Lead a guided meditation session focusing on breath awareness or body scan techniques. Help prisoners cultivate present-moment awareness and inner peace.

Step 5: Closing and Reflection

- *Closing Poses:* Conclude the session with gentle stretches or a seated meditation posture to transition back to awareness.
- *Reflection and Feedback:* Allow time for prisoners to reflect on their experiences. Invite them to share insights or observations from the practice.
- *Express Gratitude:* Encourage gratitude for the opportunity to practice yoga and acknowledge their efforts towards personal growth and rehabilitation.

Step 6: Integration and Continuation

- *Encourage Regular Practice:* Advocate for regular yoga sessions as part of a holistic rehabilitation program. Provide resources or handouts on yoga techniques for individual practice.

- *Monitor Progress:* Track participants' physical and emotional improvements over time. Document any changes in behaviour or attitude towards rehabilitation efforts.

Additional Considerations

- *Safety Guidelines:* Ensure proper alignment and safety precautions during yoga sessions, especially if prisoners have physical limitations or health concerns.
- *Instructor Qualifications:* If possible, engage certified yoga instructors or trained facilitators with experience in working with diverse populations, including prisoners.
- *Adaptability:* Modify practices based on the needs and abilities of participants. Offer variations or adjustments to accommodate individual challenges or physical conditions.

By following this step-by-step guide, correctional facilities can effectively integrate Yogic Practices into their rehabilitation programmes, fostering a supportive environment for prisoners' physical, mental, and emotional well-being.

16

Yoga for Health Management

Different Lifestyle Disorders

Yoga, an ancient practice originating from India, has gained global recognition for its profound impact on physical, mental, and emotional well-being. In the context of managing lifestyle disorders, which encompass a range of conditions influenced by unhealthy habits and modern-day stresses, yoga emerges as a holistic and therapeutic approach. By integrating physical postures (*asanas*), controlled breathing techniques (*pranayama*), and meditation, yoga offers a comprehensive toolkit for addressing the root causes and symptoms of various lifestyle-related health issues. From cardiovascular diseases to metabolic disorders, stress-related ailments, and beyond, yoga provides valuable benefits that promote overall health and enhance quality of life.

Holistic Approach of Yoga

Yoga's effectiveness lies in its ability to address the interconnectedness of body, mind, and spirit. Unlike conventional treatments that often focus solely on symptomatic relief, yoga aims for holistic healing by nurturing balance and harmony within the individual. Through regular practice, practitioners not only experience improvements in physical fitness and flexibility but also gain tools for managing stress, improving sleep quality, and fostering mental clarity. This integrative approach makes yoga a versatile and accessible option for individuals seeking to manage and prevent lifestyle disorders, offering sustainable benefits that extend beyond the yoga mat into everyday life.

Challenges of Common-man in Managing Health

Managing health effectively can be challenging for many individuals due to various factors that impact lifestyle and well-being. Here are some common challenges people face:

- *Lack of Time:* Busy schedules with work, family responsibilities, and social commitments often leave little time for exercise, meal planning, and self-care.
- *Unhealthy Eating Habits:* Easy access to processed foods, fast food options, and snacks high in sugar and fat can contribute to poor dietary choices and nutritional deficiencies.
- *Sedentary Lifestyle:* Jobs that require long hours of sitting, coupled with limited physical activity during leisure time, can lead to weight gain, muscle weakness, and cardiovascular issues.
- *Stress and Mental Health:* Pressures from work, finances, relationships, and societal expectations can lead to chronic stress, anxiety, depression, and poor coping mechanisms.
- *Lack of Access to Healthcare:* Limited access to affordable healthcare services, including preventive care and specialised treatments, can hinder timely diagnosis and management of health conditions.
- *Financial Constraints:* The cost of healthy foods, gym memberships, and medical treatments may be prohibitive for some individuals, impacting their ability to maintain optimal health.
- *Information Overload:* Conflicting health advice from media, friends, and online sources can make it difficult to make informed decisions about diet, exercise, and treatment options.
- *Motivation and Discipline:* Sticking to a healthy routine requires consistent effort, motivation, and discipline, which can be challenging to maintain over time.

Addressing these challenges often requires a multifaceted approach that includes education, lifestyle modifications, support networks, and access to affordable healthcare services. By understanding these obstacles, individuals can take proactive steps towards improving their health and well-being.

Challenges that People Face with Lifestyle Disorders

People facing lifestyle disorders encounter several challenges that can significantly impact their quality of life and overall well-being. These challenges include:

- *Difficulty in Behavior Change:* Adopting and maintaining healthy behaviours such as regular exercise, balanced nutrition, and stress management can be challenging due to ingrained habits, lack of motivation, or environmental factors.

- *Compliance with Treatment Plans:* Managing lifestyle disorders often requires adherence to medication regimens, dietary restrictions, and lifestyle modifications, which can be demanding and require sustained effort.
- *Impact on Mental Health:* Lifestyle disorders such as diabetes, obesity, and cardiovascular diseases can contribute to stress, anxiety, and depression, affecting mental well-being and complicating overall management.
- *Financial Burden:* Costs associated with medications, medical consultations, specialized diets, and lifestyle programmes can pose a financial strain, particularly for individuals with limited resources or inadequate insurance coverage.
- *Social and Psychological Effects:* Coping with the stigma associated with certain lifestyle disorders, managing social relationships amidst dietary restrictions or physical limitations, and maintaining self-esteem can be challenging.
- *Access to Healthcare Services:* Disparities in healthcare access, including availability of specialists, diagnostic tests, and preventive care, can hinder timely diagnosis and management of lifestyle disorders.
- *Risk of Complications:* Untreated or poorly managed lifestyle disorders can lead to serious complications such as heart disease, stroke, kidney failure, and nerve damage, increasing the overall burden on individuals and healthcare systems.
- *Educational Barriers:* Understanding the complexities of managing lifestyle disorders, interpreting medical advice, and navigating healthcare systems can be daunting, particularly for individuals with low health literacy or limited access to information.

Addressing these challenges requires a comprehensive approach that includes patient education, support from healthcare professionals, community resources, and policy initiatives aimed at promoting healthy lifestyles and reducing health disparities. By addressing these challenges proactively, individuals can better manage lifestyle disorders and improve their overall health outcomes.

What are Lifestyle Disorders?

Lifestyle disorders, also known as non-communicable diseases (NCDs), are health conditions primarily caused by unhealthy habits and lifestyle choices rather than infectious agents. These disorders develop over time due to factors such as poor diet, lack of physical activity, tobacco use, excessive alcohol consumption, and chronic stress. They are often preventable through lifestyle modifications and can significantly impact an individual's long-term health and quality of life.

Types of Lifestyle Disorders

- *Cardiovascular Diseases:* Including hypertension (high blood pressure), coronary artery disease, and stroke.
- *Type 2 Diabetes:* Often associated with obesity and insulin resistance.
- *Obesity:* Excessive body weight due to an imbalance between calories consumed and calories expended.
- *Chronic Respiratory Diseases:* Such as chronic obstructive pulmonary disease (COPD) and asthma, often exacerbated by smoking and environmental factors.
- *Cancer:* Certain types of cancer, such as lung, colorectal, and breast cancer, are influenced by lifestyle factors such as smoking, diet, and physical activity.
- *Metabolic Syndrome:* A cluster of conditions including high blood pressure, high blood sugar levels, excess body fat around the waist, and abnormal cholesterol levels.
- *Mental Health Disorders:* Such as depression and anxiety, which can be influenced by chronic stress and lifestyle factors.

Managing Lifestyle Disorders with Yoga

Yoga offers a holistic approach to managing lifestyle disorders by addressing physical, mental, and emotional aspects of health. Here's how yoga can help:

- *Physical Benefits:* Yoga *asanas* (postures) improve flexibility, strength, and balance. Practices like Sun Salutations (*Surya Namaskar*) and standing poses (e.g., Warrior poses) promote cardiovascular health, muscle tone, and joint mobility.
- *Stress Reduction: Pranayama* (breathing techniques) and meditation in yoga help reduce stress hormones like cortisol and promote relaxation. This can lower blood pressure, improve heart rate variability, and enhance overall mental well-being.
- *Weight Management:* Regular yoga practice can aid in weight loss and weight management by increasing metabolism, improving digestion, and promoting mindful eating habits.

- *Blood Sugar Regulation:* Yoga practices such as forward bends and twists stimulate abdominal organs, improve insulin sensitivity, and help regulate blood sugar levels in individuals with diabetes.
- *Improving Sleep Quality:* Relaxation techniques in yoga, particularly before bedtime, can promote better sleep patterns, which is crucial for overall health and managing chronic conditions.
- *Enhancing Self-awareness:* Mindfulness practices in yoga cultivate awareness of body sensations, emotions, and triggers for unhealthy behaviours, empowering individuals to make conscious lifestyle choices.
- *Supporting Mental Health:* Yoga's focus on mindfulness and breathing can reduce symptoms of anxiety, depression, and mood disorders, enhancing psychological resilience and well-being.

Integrating yoga into daily life as part of a balanced approach that includes a healthy diet, regular exercise, and medical treatment as needed can effectively manage lifestyle disorders. Consultation with healthcare professionals is essential for developing a personalised approach to managing specific health conditions through yoga and other lifestyle modifications.

Yoga — Best Remedy to Manage Lifestyle Disorders

Yoga stands out as a powerful and holistic remedy for managing lifestyle disorders, offering a multifaceted approach that addresses the root causes and symptoms of these conditions. Here's how yoga serves as an effective remedy:

Physical Benefits of Yoga

- *Improves Cardiovascular Health:* Yoga *asanas* such as Sun Salutations (Surya Namaskar) and dynamic poses like Warrior sequences promote circulation, strengthen the heart, and lower blood pressure, reducing the risk of cardiovascular diseases.
- *Enhances Flexibility and Strength:* Regular practice of yoga postures increases flexibility in muscles and joints while building strength, improving overall physical fitness and reducing the risk of injuries.
- *Aids in Weight Management:* Yoga helps burn calories, build lean muscle mass, and improve metabolism through active poses and sequences. It also encourages mindful eating habits, supporting sustainable weight loss and management.

Mental and Emotional Benefits of Yoga

- *Reduces Stress and Anxiety:* Yoga's emphasis on deep breathing (*pranayama*) and relaxation techniques triggers the parasympathetic nervous system, lowering cortisol levels and promoting relaxation, which is essential for managing stress-related disorders.
- *Promotes Mental Clarity and Focus:* Meditation and mindfulness practices in yoga enhance concentration, cognitive function, and emotional resilience, helping individuals cope with daily challenges and improve overall mental well-being.

Lifestyle Modification and Prevention

- *Encourages Healthy Habits:* Yoga fosters self-discipline and mindfulness, motivating individuals to adopt healthier lifestyles by making conscious choices in diet, exercise, and stress management.
- *Supports Long-term Health:* By reducing risk factors such as obesity, hypertension, and high cholesterol levels, yoga plays a preventive role in lifestyle-related diseases, potentially delaying or preventing their onset.

Integrative Approach to Well-being

- *Holistic Healing:* Yoga's holistic approach addresses the interconnectedness of body, mind, and spirit, promoting overall harmony and well-being. It supports individuals in managing chronic conditions while enhancing their quality of life.
- *Accessible and Adaptable:* Yoga can be practiced by people of all ages and fitness levels, making it accessible for individuals with varying health conditions and physical abilities. It can be adapted to suit specific needs and therapeutic goals.

Yoga emerges as the best remedy for lifestyle disorders by integrating physical fitness, mental clarity, and emotional balance. Its therapeutic benefits extend beyond symptom management to empower individuals to take proactive steps towards healthier living and preventing chronic diseases. Embracing yoga as part of a comprehensive health management strategy offers a pathway to sustainable well-being and improved quality of life for individuals seeking to overcome lifestyle-related challenges.

Developing a specific Yogic protocol to manage lifestyle disorders involves integrating yoga practices that address the physical, mental, and emotional aspects of health. Here's a structured protocol tailored to manage common lifestyle disorders:

Yogic Protocol for Managing Lifestyle Disorders

General Guidelines:

- *Consistency:* Practice yoga regularly, ideally 3–5 times a week, to experience cumulative benefits.
- *Mindfulness:* Approach each session with awareness of breath, body sensations, and mental state.
- *Progression:* Start with beginner-friendly poses and gradually advance based on individual comfort and ability.

Warm-up and Pranayama:

- *Duration:* 5–10 minutes
- *Purpose:* Prepare the body and mind for yoga practice, enhance circulation, and promote relaxation.
- *Practices:*
  - *Dirga Pranayama (Three-Part Breath):* Deep inhalation into the abdomen, chest, and upper lungs, followed by slow exhalation.
  - *Bhastrika Pranayama (Bellows Breath):* Rapid and forceful inhalation and exhalation through the nose, energising the body and improving oxygenation.

Yoga Asanas (Postures):

- *Duration:* 20–30 minutes
- *Purpose:* Improve flexibility, strength, and balance, and address specific health concerns associated with lifestyle disorders.
- *Recommended Asanas:*
  - *Tadasana (Mountain Pose):* Grounding and improves posture.
  - *Virabhadrasana series (Warrior Poses):* Strengthens legs, core muscles, and enhances stamina.
  - *Uttanasana (Standing Forward Bend):* Stretches hamstrings, calms the mind, and relieves stress.
  - *Setu Bandhasana (Bridge Pose):* Opens chest, improves spinal flexibility, and stimulates thyroid gland function.
  - *Bhujangasana (Cobra Pose):* Strengthens back muscles, stimulates abdominal organs, and improves digestion.

Relaxation and Meditation:

- *Duration:* 10–15 minutes
- *Purpose:* Promote mental calmness, reduce stress, and enhance overall well-being.

- *Practices:*
  - *Savasana (Corpse Pose):* Complete relaxation, allowing the body and mind to rest deeply.
  - *Guided Meditation:* Focuses on mindfulness, positive affirmations, or visualization techniques to cultivate inner peace and clarity.

Closing and Reflection:

- *Duration:* 5 minutes
- *Purpose:* Integrate the benefits of the practice, express gratitude, and set intentions for health and well-being.
- *Practices:*
  - *Pranayama:* Conclude with gentle breathing exercises to balance energy.
  - *Reflection:* Invite participants to journal or mentally reflect on their experience, noting any physical, mental, or emotional changes.

Additional Considerations

- *Consultation:* Individuals with specific health concerns should consult healthcare providers before beginning a yoga practice, especially if managing chronic conditions or recovering from injuries.
- *Adaptability:* Modify poses and practices as needed to accommodate individual abilities, health conditions, and comfort levels.
- *Progress Tracking:* Monitor progress in flexibility, strength, stress levels, and overall well-being to assess the effectiveness of the Yogic protocol.

By following this Yogic protocol consistently and mindfully, individuals can effectively manage lifestyle disorders while enhancing their overall health and well-being. Regular practice not only addresses physical symptoms but also supports mental clarity, emotional resilience, and holistic healing.

In conclusion, Yogic management offers a transformative approach to addressing lifestyle disorders by integrating physical postures, breathing techniques, and meditation practices that promote holistic well-being. Through regular and mindful practice, individuals can experience profound improvements in their physical health, mental clarity, and emotional balance.

Yoga's focus on mindfulness and self-awareness empowers individuals to make conscious lifestyle choices, leading to sustainable health outcomes. By reducing stress levels, improving flexibility, and enhancing overall fitness, yoga becomes a versatile tool for preventing and managing conditions such as cardiovascular diseases, diabetes, obesity, and mental health disorders.

Furthermore, the adaptability of yoga makes it accessible to people of all ages and fitness levels, offering a personalized approach to health management. Whether practiced in a group setting or individually, yoga fosters a sense of empowerment and resilience, supporting individuals on their journey to optimal health and a balanced lifestyle. Embracing Yogic principles not only addresses the symptoms of lifestyle disorders but also cultivates a lasting foundation for lifelong well-being and vitality.

17

Yoga for Aged People

Yoga offers profound benefits for people of all ages, including older adults who aim to maintain or improve their physical health, mental well-being, and overall quality of life. As individuals age, they may face unique challenges such as reduced mobility, joint stiffness, balance issues, and cognitive changes. Yoga provides a gentle yet effective approach to address these challenges, promoting flexibility, strength, relaxation, and inner peace.

Introduction to Yoga for Older Adults

Yoga is an ancient practice that includes physical postures (*asanas*), breathing techniques (*pranayama*), and meditation to harmonise the body, mind, and spirit. For seniors, yoga serves as a versatile tool for maintaining mobility, managing chronic conditions, and enhancing mental clarity. Its gentle approach makes it accessible to individuals with varying levels of physical ability, ensuring that everyone can participate and benefit.

We'll explore how yoga can be tailored to meet the specific needs of older adults, emphasising its role in promoting physical health, mental well-being, and a sense of connection to oneself and others. Through regular practice, seniors can experience improved flexibility, better balance, reduced stress levels, and a renewed sense of vitality, making yoga a valuable companion on their journey towards healthy aging.

Challenges Aged Facing

Older adults face a range of challenges that can impact their daily lives and overall well-being. These challenges include:

- *Physical Health Issues:* Aging often brings about physical health challenges such as joint stiffness, decreased flexibility, muscle weakness, and chronic conditions like arthritis, osteoporosis, and cardiovascular disease. These conditions can affect mobility and independence.

- *Cognitive Changes:* Some older adults may experience cognitive decline, memory loss, and difficulties with concentration and decision-making, which can impact daily activities and quality of life.
- *Social Isolation:* Loss of friends and family members, retirement, and physical limitations can lead to social isolation and loneliness, which are linked to poorer health outcomes and mental well-being.
- *Financial Concerns:* Managing fixed incomes, healthcare expenses, and navigating insurance and retirement benefits can be challenging, especially for those on limited budgets.
- *Mental Health Issues:* Depression, anxiety, and stress can affect older adults, often exacerbated by life transitions, health problems, or social isolation.
- *Caregiving Responsibilities:* Many older adults may find themselves in caregiving roles for spouses, children, or other family members, which can be physically and emotionally demanding.
- *Access to Healthcare:* Accessing healthcare services, including transportation to appointments, affordability of medications, and understanding complex medical information, can be challenging for seniors.
- *Nutrition and Lifestyle:* Maintaining a healthy diet, engaging in regular exercise, and managing chronic conditions through lifestyle changes can be challenging as individuals age.

Addressing these challenges requires a combination of support from family and community, access to healthcare services, opportunities for social engagement, and resources for maintaining physical and mental well-being. Strategies such as regular exercise, social activities, cognitive stimulation, and mindfulness practices like yoga can play a crucial role in enhancing the quality of life for older adults.

Psycho-physiological Health Issues

Older adults often face a variety of health issues that can affect their quality of life and require on-going management. Some common health issues among the elderly include:

- *Chronic Conditions:* Many seniors live with chronic diseases such as hypertension (high blood pressure), diabetes, arthritis, osteoporosis, and heart disease. These conditions require careful management to prevent complications and maintain overall health.

- *Mobility Problems:* Reduced muscle strength, joint stiffness, and balance issues can lead to mobility problems and an increased risk of falls, which is a significant concern for older adults.
- *Cognitive Decline:* Age-related cognitive changes, including mild cognitive impairment and dementia (such as Alzheimer's disease), can affect memory, reasoning, and decision-making abilities.
- *Sensory Impairments:* Hearing loss, vision problems (like cataracts or age-related macular degeneration), and diminished sense of taste or smell can impact daily functioning and quality of life.
- *Mental Health Issues:* Depression and anxiety are common among older adults, often due to factors such as social isolation, chronic illness, bereavement, or changes in life circumstances.
- *Nutritional Challenges:* Poor appetite, difficulty chewing or swallowing, and inadequate nutrition can lead to malnutrition and weight loss, which are prevalent concerns among seniors.
- *Medication Management:* Older adults often take multiple medications for various health conditions, increasing the risk of medication interactions, side effects, and medication non-adherence.
- *Urinary and Bowel Issues:* Incontinence, urinary tract infections (UTIs), constipation, and other digestive issues become more prevalent with age and can impact daily comfort and quality of life.
- *Skin Problems:* Aging skin is more susceptible to dryness, bruising, pressure sores, and skin infections, requiring careful skincare and preventive measures.
- *End-of-Life Care:* Many older adults face decisions about end-of-life care preferences, palliative care, and managing chronic illnesses in their later years.

Managing these health issues requires a comprehensive approach that includes regular medical check-ups, medication management, healthy lifestyle habits (including diet and exercise), social engagement, and access to supportive care services. By addressing these challenges proactively, older adults can maintain their independence, quality of life, and overall well-being as they age.

Yogic Package for Aged People

Creating a Yogic package for older adults involves designing a program that addresses their unique needs, promotes physical health, mental clarity, and emotional well-being. Here's a structured Yogic package tailored for aged individuals:

Warm-up and Pranayama (5–10 minutes):

- *Purpose:* Prepare the body and mind for yoga practice, enhance circulation, and promote relaxation.
- *Practices:*
  - *Dirga Pranayama (Three-Part Breath):* Deep inhalation into the abdomen, chest, and upper lungs, followed by slow exhalation.
  - *Bhramari Pranayama (Humming Bee Breath):* Calms the mind, reduces stress, and enhances concentration.

Gentle Yoga Asanas (20–30 minutes):

- *Purpose:* Improve flexibility, enhance joint mobility, and strengthen muscles with gentle poses that accommodate older adults' abilities.
- *Recommended Asanas:*
  - *Tadasana (Mountain Pose):* Improves posture and balance.
  - *Vrikshasana (Tree Pose):* Enhances balance and stability.
  - *Baddha Konasana (Bound Angle Pose):* Opens hips and improves flexibility.
  - *Setu Bandhasana (Bridge Pose):* Strengthens back muscles and improves spinal flexibility.
  - *Supta Matsyendrasana (Supine Spinal Twist):* Increases spinal mobility and releases tension in the back.
  - *Savasana (Corpse Pose):* Promotes deep relaxation and rejuvenation.

Mindfulness Meditation (10–15 minutes):

- *Purpose:* Cultivate mental clarity, reduce stress, and promote overall well-being.
- *Practices:*
  - *Guided Meditation:* Focuses on relaxation, gratitude, or visualisation to enhance mental and emotional resilience.
  - *Body Scan Meditation:* Brings awareness to different parts of the body, promoting relaxation and mindfulness.

Closing and Pranayama (5 minutes):

- *Purpose:* Integrate the benefits of the practice, express gratitude, and promote inner peace.
- *Practices:*
  - *Anulom Vilom Pranayama* (Alternate Nostril Breathing): Balances energy channels and calms the mind.
  - *Reflection:* Invite participants to reflect on their practice and set intentions for health and well-being.

Additional Considerations

- *Adaptability:* Modify poses and practices as needed to accommodate individual abilities and health conditions.
- *Safety:* Emphasize proper alignment and provide support (such as props or chairs) for stability during poses.
- *Progress Tracking:* Encourage participants to monitor improvements in flexibility, strength, and overall well-being over time.

This Yogic package for older adults offers a gentle yet effective approach to promoting physical fitness, mental clarity, and emotional balance. Regular practice can enhance mobility, reduce stress, and contribute to a fulfilling and healthy lifestyle as individuals age gracefully.

Yoga stands as a profound remedy for older adults, offering a holistic approach to enhance physical health, mental clarity, and emotional well-being. Tailored to address the specific needs and challenges of aging, yoga provides a versatile toolkit that supports seniors in maintaining vitality and quality of life.

Physical Benefits of Yoga for Older Adults

Yoga's Gentle Yet Effective Postures (asanas) Promote

- *Flexibility and Mobility:* Gentle stretches and poses improve joint flexibility and range of motion, reducing stiffness and enhancing overall mobility.
- *Strength and Balance:* Weight-bearing poses strengthen muscles and bones, crucial for maintaining balance and reducing the risk of falls.
- *Pain Relief:* Yoga's therapeutic poses alleviate chronic pain associated with conditions like arthritis, promoting comfort and ease of movement.

Mental and Emotional Well-being

Yoga Practices such as

- *Pranayama (Breathing Techniques):* Deep breathing exercises calm the mind, reduce stress, and enhance cognitive function, fostering mental clarity and emotional resilience.
- *Meditation:* Mindfulness meditation cultivates inner peace, reduces anxiety, and improves concentration, promoting a positive outlook and emotional balance.

Holistic Health Promotion

Yoga's Holistic Approach Encompasses

- *Heart Health:* Practices like gentle flow sequences and relaxation techniques lower blood pressure, improve circulation, and support cardiovascular health.
- *Digestive Health:* Yoga poses stimulate digestion, relieve constipation, and promote gastrointestinal function, enhancing overall well-being.
- *Sleep Quality:* Relaxation techniques and bedtime yoga sequences promote restful sleep, essential for rejuvenation and vitality.

Integrative and Accessible Practice

Yoga's Adaptability Makes it Accessible to All Older Adults

- *Modifications:* Poses can be modified with props or chairs to accommodate varying levels of mobility and physical ability.
- *Community and Connection:* Group yoga classes foster social interaction, combatting loneliness and promoting a sense of belonging and community support.

In conclusion, yoga emerges as an ideal remedy for older adults by nurturing physical vitality, mental clarity, and emotional well-being. Its gentle yet impactful practices empower seniors to age gracefully, maintaining independence and enjoying a fulfilling quality of life. Embracing yoga as part of a regular wellness routine offers older adults a pathway to holistic health, resilience, and a renewed sense of vitality in their golden years.

The benefits of yoga practice for older adults extend far beyond physical fitness, encompassing mental clarity, emotional well-being, and overall quality of life. Through its gentle yet effective techniques, yoga offers a holistic approach that addresses the unique challenges of aging while promoting vitality and resilience.

Physically, yoga enhances flexibility, strength, and balance, crucial for maintaining mobility and reducing the risk of falls. It alleviates joint stiffness, improves posture, and supports bone health, enabling older adults to move with greater ease and confidence in their daily activities.

Mentally and emotionally, yoga cultivates mindfulness, reduces stress, and enhances cognitive function, promoting mental clarity and emotional resilience. By integrating deep breathing exercises and meditation, yoga empowers seniors to manage anxiety, depression, and the emotional challenges that may accompany aging.

Furthermore, yoga's integrative approach supports overall health by improving cardiovascular function, digestion, and sleep quality. Its adaptability ensures accessibility for individuals of all abilities, fostering inclusivity and a sense of community among older adults practicing together.

Embracing yoga as a regular part of their wellness routine enables older adults to age gracefully, maintain independence, and enjoy a fulfilling life. By harnessing the transformative power of yoga, seniors can navigate the aging process with strength, vitality, and a profound sense of well-being, making yoga an invaluable tool for holistic health and longevity.

References

Acharya, Sriram Sharma (2003): *Yagya Ek Samgra Upchar Prakriya.Vol. 26*. Akhand Jyoti Sansthan, Mathura; UP, India, pp. 27.

Akiskal, HS; Benazzi, F (May 2006). "The DSM-IV and ICD-10 categories of recurrent [major] depressive and bipolar II disorders: evidence that they lie on a dimensional spectrum". J Affect Disorder 92 (1): 45–54.

Ansel Woldt, Sarah Toman (eds) (2005). *Gestalt Therapy History, Theory, and Practice*. Gestalt Press. ISBN 0-7619-2791-3 (pbk.).

Anthony, Roth and Peter Fonagy (2005), *What Works for Whom? A Critical Review of Psychotherapy Research*, Guilford Press, ISBN 572306505

Anthony, Roth; Peter, Fonagy (2005). *What Works for Whom? A Critical Review of Psychotherapy Research*, Guilford Press, ISBN 572306505

Anvita Singh, V.P. Sharma, J.K. Trivedi, Rakesh Shukla, Sunita Tiwari & Kamakhya Kumar Yogic Practices can improve the bladder functions in incomplete spinal injury patients, Reviews of Progress: *International weekly Medical Research Journal*, Vol. 1 Issue: 22, 25 Sept. 2013. pp. 1–5.

Aurobindo, Sri (1993). The integral yoga. Sri Aurobindo Ashram publication department.

Aziz, Robert (2007), The Syndetic Paradigm: The Untrodden Path Beyond Freud and Jung, a refereed publication of The State University of New York Press. ISBN 13:978-0-7914-6982-8.

Bateman, A. and Holmes, J. (1995). *Introduction to Psychoanalysis: Contemporary Theory and Practice*. Routledge. ISBN 0-415-10739-3.

Bateman, Anthony; Brown, Dennis and Pedder, Jonathan (2000). *Introduction to Psychotherapy: An Outline of Psychodynamic Principles and Practice*". Routledge. ISBN 0-415-20569-7.

Bhogle, S. & Jai Prakash, I. (1993) Indicators of subjective well-being in a non-clinical sample. *Psychological Studies*, 38 (3), 135–141.

Bhole MV. 1981; Yogic treatment of bronchial asthma – A medical report. *Yoga Mimamsa 1981*; 20, pp. 1–12.

Bhushan, L.I. (1994) A yogic model of mental health. *Indian Journal of Psychological Issues*, 1 (3), 1–5.

Birkenholz, Robert J. (1999) *Effective Adult Learning*. Interstate Publishers. p. 91.

Chandrakar, R., Kumar, K., & Chandrakar, P., A Study on the Effect of Integrated Yoga on Labor Pain; *International Journal of Yoga and Allied Sciences*, Vol. 6, No. 1, 2017. pp. 10–16.

Chandrakar, R., Kumar, K., & Chandrakar, P., To Study the Effect of Integrated Yoga Practices on Stress during Pregnancy, *Imperial Journal of Interdisciplinary research*, Vol: 2, Issue: 9, 2016. pp. 908–13, ISSN: 2454-1362.

Chandrakar, R., Kumar, K., & Verma, S., The psycho-spiritual effects of Punsavan sanskara on pregnant mother and foetus, *International Journal of Science and Consciousness*, Vol: 2, Issue 3 Aug 2016 pp. 01–12. ISSN:2455-2038.

Clark, LA (2007). "Assessment and diagnosis of personality disorder: perennial issues and an emerging reconceptualization". *Annual Review Psychol* 58: 227–57.

Crocker, Sylvia (1999). *A Well-Lived Life, Essays in Gestalt Therapy*. SAGE Publications. ISBN 0-88163-287-2 (pbk.).

Daftuar and Sharma (1997). *Psychology of wellbeing*. Global Vision Publishing House, New Delhi, p. 363.

Dalal, A. S.(2001). *Psychology, mental health and yoga*. Sri Aurobindo Ashram Press, Pondicherry

Datey, K.K. (1978). Yoga: prevention and management of hypertension. *Swasth Hind*, 22, 56–58.

Davidson RJ et al. 2003 Alterations in Brain and Immune Function Produced by Mindfulness Meditation, *Psychosomatic Medicine* (Jul-Aug) 65 (4), pp. 564–70.

Davies T. (May 1997). "ABC of mental health. Mental health assessment". BMJ 314 (7093): 1536–9.

Davis, K L (1989) Serotoner-gic studies in patients with affective and personality dirsor- ders. *Arch. Gen. Psychiatry* 46, 587–599.

Devi P & Kumar K; A Study on the Effect of Yogic Innervation at Haemoglobin Level among the College going Girls; *International Journal of Yoga and Allied Sciences*, Vol. 11, No. 1, 2022, pp. 36–45.

Divekar, M.V. (1982). Yoga therapy for diabetes and obesity. *Yoga*, 20 (6), 19–29.

Dr A S Dalal (2001) *A Greater Psychology: An Introduction to Sri Aurobindo's Psychological Thought*, Jeremy P Tarcher/Putnam, p. 55

Dr Pranav Pandya (2004) The Occult Science of Upasana, *Akhand Jyoti*, Sept.- Oct 2004, p. 27.

Ellenberger, Henri F. (1970). *The Discovery of the Unconscious: The History and Evolution of Dynamic Psychiatry*. Basic Books.

Emerson Ralph Waldo 1860, *The Conduct of Life*, Ticknor and Fields, Boston, pp. 145–172.

Emerson, Ralph Waldo (1860) *The Conduct of Life*, p. 258.

Exploring the therapeutic effects of yoga and its ability to increase quality of life. (n.d.) retrieved June 16, 2024, from www.ncbi.nlm.nih.gov/pmc/articles/PMC3193654/

Fiske, D.W. (1949). Consistency of the factorial structures of personality ratings from different sources. *Journal of Abnormal Social Psychology*, 44, 329–344.

Frank, Jerome (1988) "What is Psychotherapy?". In Bloch, Sidney *(ed.). An Introduction to the Psychotherapies.* Oxford: Oxford University Press. pp. 1–2.

Freedman, J. (1978). *Happy people: What happiness is, who has it, and why*. New York: Harcourt Brace Jovanovich, pp. 23.

Funder, DC (2004) Personality and Life Satishfaction: A Facet level Analysis, *Personality and Social Psychology Bulletin*, (30), pp. 1062–75.

Gamma A, Angst J, Ajdacic V, Eich D, Rössler W (March 2007). "The spectra of neurasthenia and depression: course, stability and transitions". *Eur Arch Psychiatry Clin Neurosis* 257 (2): 120–7.

Gazzaniga, M.S., & Heatherton, T.F. (2006). *Psychological Science*. New York: W.W. Norton & Company, Inc.

Goldberg, L. R. (1981) Language and individual differences: The search for universals in personality lexicons. In L. Wheeler (Ed.), *Review of Personality and Social Psychology, Vol. 2*. Beverly Hills, CA: Sage.

Gordon Willard Allport (1937). *The American Journal of Psychology*, 50, pp. 141–156.

Hans Eysenck, (1991). Dimensions of personality: 16: 5 or 3? Criteria for a taxonomic paradigm. *Personality and Individual Differences*, 12, 773–790.

Hans, Strupp and Jeffrey Binder (1984). *Psychotherapy in a New Key*. New York, Basic Books, ISBN 9780465067473

Herbert Benson, (1972) 'The physiology of meditation', *Scientific American*, Vol. 226, No. 2, pp. 84–90

Hostman Judith 2005 The Scientific American Brave New Brain, *Scientific American* p. 31

James Austin (1998) *Zen and the Brain*. Cambridge: MIT Press. Boston, p. 78

Jangid, R.K., Vyas, J.N. & Shukla, T.R. (1988). Effect of transcendental meditation in cases of anxiety neurosis. *Indian Journal of Clinical Psychology*, 15, 77–79.

John D. Mayer. (2007) Asserting the Definition of Personality, The Online Newsletter for Personality Science. Issue 1, Spring 2007, pp. 1–4.

Joshi, Rajani R.(2006): *The Integrated Science of Yagna*, Yug Nirman Yojna, Gayatri Tapobhumi, Mathura. p. 186.

Judith Horstman 2005, The Scientific American Brave New Brain, *Scientific American,* p. 52

K.V. Belsare (1989) *Santanche Atmacharitra*, Second edition, Tridal Publishers, Mumbai, pp. 210.

Kakkar D & Kumar K; Effect of Bhoot Suddhi Kriya on EEG Alpha; *Yoga Mimansa*, Kaivalyadham Lonavala, Maharastra, Vol. 43, No. 4. pp. 310–15.

Kamakhya Kumar & Ajay Bharadwaj; *Human Consciousness and Yogic Science*, 2016.

Kamakhya Kumar; *A Handbook of Yoga Nidra*, D K Printworld, Delhi; 2013.

Kamakhya Kumar; *Super Science of Yoga*, Standard Publishers India, New Delhi; 2008.

Kamakhya Kumar; *Yoga Education: A Text Book*, Shipra Publication, Delhi; 2012.

Kamakhya Kumar; *Yoga Psychology: A Handbook of Yogic Psychotherapy*; D K Printworld, Delhi; 2013.

Kashner TM, Rush AJ, Surís A, et al (May 2003). "Impact of structured clinical interviews on physicians' practices in community mental health settings". *Psychiatric Service*. 54 (5): 712–8.

Kaul, H. Kumar (1993). *Yoga and Drug Addiction*. B.R. Pub. Corp. p. 92

Kaur, P., & Sinha, A. K. (*1992*). Dimensions of guna in organizational setting, *Vikalpa*, 17, 27–32.

Kinderman P, Lobban F (2000). "Evolving formulations: Sharing complex information with clients". *Behavioral and Cognitive Psychotherapy,* 28 (3): 307–10.

Kothari A & Kumar K; Physiological Benefits of Yoga for College Students; *International Journal of Yoga and Allied Sciences*, Vol. 11, No. 1, 2022, pp. 70–76.

Kumar K & Joshi B; Study on the Effect of Pranakarshan Pranayama & Yoga Nidra on Alpha EEG & GSR.; *Indian Journal of Traditional Knowledge*; NISCAIR, New Delhi Vol. 8, No. 3 July 2009. pp. 453–454.

Kumar K & Kulsrestha A; Laghu Samkha Prakshalana: Is It an Influential factor in General Health Status; *Yoga Mimansa*, Kaivalyadham Lonavala, Maharastra Vol. 42 No. 4, Jan. 2011.

Kumar K & Tiwary S; Academic Anxiety among Student and the Management through Yoga; *International Journal of Yoga and Allied Sciences*, Vol. 3, No. 1, 2014. pp. 50–53. ISSN: 2278-5159

Kumar K & Tripathy V; Phenomenal aspects of Immunity in Vedic Science and Approach of Yoga in Present Scenario; *International Journal of Yoga and Allied Sciences*, Vol. 11, No. 1, 2022, pp. 5–11.

Kumar K, A study on the effect of Yogic Intervention on Occupational stress level of Working Women; *International Journal of Yoga and Allied Sciences*, Vol. 4, No. 2, 2015. pp. 110–115. ISSN: 2278-5159

Kumar K, Approach of Yoga based lifestyle towards Social adjustment among Students, *International Journal of Yoga and Allied Sciences*, Vol. 5, No. 1, 2016. pp.18–23.

Kumar K, Effect of Yogic Intervention on General Body weight of the subjects: A study report; *International Journal of Yoga and Allied Sciences*, Vol. 4, No. 1, 2015. pp. 11–14. ISSN: 2278-5159

Kumar K, Holistic approach of Yoga, Proceedings of National Seminar on Yoga for Nation Building 27- 28 March 2019 Sponsored by ICSSR, New Delhi and Organized by Dept. of Yoga, Barkatullah University, Bhopal.

Kumar K, Origin and Application of Yoga Nidra, Proceedings of National Symposium on Healthy Yoga Lifestyle – for Prevention of Lifestyle diseases & CME Program on – Role of Yoga, Nature, Nutrition and Meditation in Promotion of Holistic Health, Arogyadham, Mahatma Gandhi Institute of Medical Sciences, Sevagram Wardha, Maharastra, 10–11 Sept 2015.

Kumar K, Phenomenon of Consciousness and its approach to Meditation, *International Journal of Science and Consciousness*, Vol. 1, Issue 1, July-Sep. 2015, pp. 7–12.

Kumar K, Reversing Hypertension through Yogic Intervention, *International Journal of Yoga and Allied Sciences*, Vol. 5, No. 2, 2016. pp. 95–100. ISSN: 2278-5159

Kumar K, Scientific Basis of Yoga; Souvenir of CME Program on Yoga: An Art of healthy living, organized by King George Medical University, Lucknow, 21st June 2015.

Kumar K, Sharma C & Kumar A; A Study on the Effect of Neti on Optic Nerve Conduction Velocity; *Yoga Mimansa*, Kaivalyadham Lonavala, Maharastra Vol. 42 No.1, April 2010.

Kumar K, Vedic Mantras: an influential factor for Spiritual Health, *International Journal of Science and Consciousness*, Vol. 1, Issue 2 Oct-Dec 2015 pp. 9–14.

Kumar K; A Holistic Approach to Stress Management; *Nature & Wealth*, Vol. VII, No. 4; Oct 2008.

Kumar K; A Study of the Effect of Yogic intervention on Anxiety among Youth, Souvenir of National Yoga Week 2014; Organized by Morarji Desai National Institute of Yoga, New Delhi between 12–18 Feb 14. pp. 23–25.

Kumar K; A Study of the Effect of Yogic intervention on Blood uric acid Level in Gout Patients; *International Journal of Yoga and Allied Sciences*, Vol. 2, No. 2, 2013. pp. 104–108. ISSN: 2278-5159

Kumar K; A study of the improvement of physical mental health through Yoga nidra; *Dev Sanskriti Inter-disciplinary Research Journal*, Vol. 4, Issue 4; (2006) 39–46.

Kumar K; A Study on Effect of Yogic Intervention on Adjustment Level of Working Women; *International Journal of Yoga and Allied Sciences*, Vol. 6, No. 2, 2017. pp. 149–155.

Kumar K; A Study on the Effect of Yogic Intervention on Anxiety, *Yoga Vijnan*, M.D.N.I.Y, New Delhi Vol. 3 (Combined Issue 1, 2, 3 & 4) 2009–10, pp. 60–63.

Kumar K; A Study on the Effect of Yogic intervention on serum glucose level on Diabetics; *International Journal of Yoga and Allied Sciences*, Indian Association of Yoga, New Delhi Vol. 1, No. 1 June 2012. pp. 68–73.

Kumar K; A study on the impact on ESR level through Yogic Relaxation Technique *Yoga nidra*; *Indian Journal of Traditional Knowledge*; NISCAIR, New Delhi Vol. 11, No. 2 Apr 2012. pp. 358–61.

Kumar K; A study on the impact on Stress & Anxiety through Yoga Nidra; *Indian Journal of Traditional Knowledge*; NISCAIR New Delhi, Vol. 7, No. 3 July 2008. pp. 405–409

Kumar K; Awakening of Kundalini through Yoga; *Nature & Wealth*, Vol. VI, No. 3; July 2007.

Kumar K; Changes in Hemoglobin among House wives through Yoga: A Pilot study; *International Journal of Yoga and Allied Sciences*, Vol. 7, No. 2, 2018, pp. 113–117.

Kumar K; Current issues in Science of Consciousness and Yoga; *International Journal of Yoga and Allied Sciences*, Vol. 3, No. 2, 2014. pp 93–97. ISSN: 2278-5159

Kumar K; Effect of Learning Music as a Practice of Nada Yoga on EEG Alpha and General Well Being; *Yoga Mimansa*, Kaivalyadham Lonavala, Maharastra Vol. 43 No. 3 2011. pp. 215–20.

Kumar K; Effect of Mantra on Mental Health; *Nature & Wealth*, Vol. VI, No. 1; Jan 2007.

Kumar K; Effect of Yoga nidra on hypertension and other psychological co-relates; *Yoga the Science Journal,* Volume 3, Issue 7; Published through Yoga Publications, Hubli, Karnataka. (2005)

Kumar K; Effect of Yogic Intervention on Adolescent's Intelligence and Well Being Souvenir of National Yoga Week Feb 2013; Organized by Morarji Desai National Institute of Yoga, New Delhi.

Kumar K; Effect of Yogic Package on the Patients of Diabetes mellitus; Souvenir of National Yoga Week 2008; Organized by Morarji Desai National Institute of Yoga, New Delhi.

Kumar K; Effect of Yogic Practices on Lipid Profile in Patients of Coronary Artery Disease; *Yoga Vijnan*, M.D.N.I.Y, New Delhi Vol. 2, Issue 1 & 2. 2008

Kumar K; Essence of Integral Yoga of Sri Aurobindo; *Nature & Wealth*, Vol. IX, No. 3; July 2010.

Kumar K; Experience Swadhyaya for Healthy Mind; *Nature & Wealth*, Vol. IX, No. 2; Apr 2010.

Kumar K; Human Mind, Mental Process and role of Yoga in Mental Health; *International Journal of Science and Consciousness*, Vol. 4, No. 2, 2018, pp. 48–54.

Kumar K; Impact of Yogic practices on General-intelligence and General-well-being of School going children; *International Journal of Yoga and Allied Sciences*, Vol. 13, No. 2, 2024.

Kumar K; Importance of Healthy Life Style in Healthy living; Juniper Online Journal of Public Health. 2017; 2(5):

Kumar K; Improving Mental Health through Mantra Yoga; *Yoga Magazine (Body Mind Spirit)*; Published from York Street, London; Issue 55, Aug. 2007, pp. 60–62.

Kumar K; Just Breath: Improve Your Respiration through Yogic Breathings; *Yoga Magazine (Body Mind Spirit)*; Published from York Street, London; Issue 53, June 2007, pp. 66–68.

Kumar K; Manage the psycho-complexities through Yoga Nidra; Proceedings of National conference on Yoga Therapy, organized at Mangalore Univ. 18–19 Jan 2013, pp. 26–31.

Kumar K; Managing the detrimental factors of aging through Yoga; *Indian Journal of Traditional Knowledge*; N I S C A I R, New Delhi Vol. 16, (suppl) June 2017. pp s96-s100.

Kumar K; Meditation it's Advantages & Application; *Nature & Wealth*, Vol. V, No. 3; July 2006.

Kumar K; Mental Distress in Corporate Persons & Its Management through Yoga; *International Journal of Yoga and Allied Sciences*, Vol. 7, No. 1, 2018, pp. 14–18.

Kumar K; Physiological Benefits of Yoga for College Students; *International Journal of Yoga and Allied Sciences*, Vol. 11, No. 1, 2022, pp. 70–76.

Kumar K; Practice of Yoga to Improve Moral Values in Children's Education System; *Nature & Wealth*, Vol. IX, No. 1; Jan 2010

Kumar K; Pragya Yoga; *Seva Chetana*, Vol. 11, No. 1 (2011), 164–166

Kumar K; Prāyashchitta Sādhanā: A Psycho-Spiritual Approach; *International Journal of Yoga and Allied Sciences*, Vol. 9, No. 1, 2020, pp. 89–94.

Kumar K; Psychological Changes as related to Yoga Nidra; *International Journal of Psychology*: A Biopsychosocial Approach Publisher: Vytautas Magnus University Lithuania 2010 (6), pp. 129–137

Kumar K; Relax Through Yoga Nidra; Nisargopchar *Varta*, Vol. 6, No. 10, 2014. pp. 30–33.

Kumar K; Reversing the ischemic heart disease through Yogic Relaxation Souvenir of National Yoga Week Feb 2010; Organized by Morarji Desai National Institute of Yoga, New Delhi.

Kumar K; Role of Yoga-nidra in Immunity Development; *International Journal of Yoga and Allied Sciences*, Vol. 9, No. 2, 2020.

Kumar K; School Going Children and Shaping their Personality Souvenir of National Yoga Week 2009; between 16–22 Feb 09 Organized by Morarji Desai National Institute of Yoga, New Delhi.

Kumar K; Self-Management through Psycho-spiritual Techniques; SEVAMED (Oct. 2011) 10 (4) pp. 1–2.

Kumar K; Significance of *Nadi Sodhan* and *Kapalbhati* on forced ventilation capacity (FVC), maximum voluntary ventilation (MVV) and picks expiratory flow rate (PEFR); *Indian Journal of Traditional Knowledge*; NISCAIR, New Delhi, Vol. 12, No. 2 Apr 2013. pp. 342–45.

Kumar K; So- Ham Meditation: Anti Stress Mechanism; *Nature & Wealth*, Vol. VIII, No. 3, July 2009.

Kumar K; Spiritual Health through Yoga; *Nature & Wealth*, Vol. VI, No. 2; Apr 2007.

Kumar K; Strengthen the Education System Through Yogic Intervention; (Book Chapter) *Yoga Education*, A.P.H Publishing Corporation, New Delhi, 2011

Kumar K; Stress free life through Yoga Nidra; Souvenir, International Symposium on Yogism (Dec 2010) 36–38

Kumar K; The Healing Sleep; *Yoga Magazine (Body Mind Spirit)*; Published from York Street, London; Issue 50 March 2007, pp. 42–44.

Kumar K; Trataka Its Importance and Application; *Nature & Wealth*, Vol. VII, No. 3, July 2008.

Kumar K; Yagyopathy: A New Dimension of Research in Therapy System; *Nature & Wealth*, Vol. X, No. 1; Mar 2011.

Kumar K; Yagyopathy: Importance and Application; *Nature & Wealth*, Vol. VIII, No. 4; Oct 2009.

Kumar K; Yoga and Human Excellence; *International Journal of Yoga and Allied Sciences*, Vol. 8, No. 1, 2019, pp. 77–81.

Kumar K; *Yoga nidra* and its impact on students wellbeing; *Yoga Mimamsa*, Kaivalyadham Lonavala, Maharastra (2004) 36 (1); 31–35.

Kumar K; Yogic Intervention and its Effect on General Well Being; *International Journal of Yoga and Allied Sciences*, Indian Association of Yoga, New Delhi, Vol. 1, No. 2 June 2012. pp. 150–155.

Kumar K; Yogic Intervention and its impact on general body weight of office going women: A control trial; *International Journal of Yoga and Allied Sciences*, Vol. 10, No. 1, 2021, pp. 5–11.

Kumar, K. & Patel, S. Influence of Yoga and Diet control in managing the state of Obesity, *Journal of Yoga and Physiology*, ISSN: 2476-1303, Vol: 1, Issue 1, Oct 2016, pp. 1–5.

Kumar, K., Naudiyal S., Practice of Nada Yoga and its Psychological benefits; *International Journal of Science and Consciousness*, Vol. 6, No. 2, 2020.

Larsen, R. J., & Buss, D. M. (2005). *Personality psychology: Domains of knowledge about human nature* (2nd ed.). Boston: McGraw-Hill. 4 p.

Lawton, M.P. (1983). The varieties of well-being. *Experimental Ageing Research*, 9, 65–72.

Maclver R M (1915) Personality and the Suprapersonal, *The Philosophical Review* Sep. 1915, Vol. 24, p. 48.

McAdams, D. P. (2006). *The person: A new introduction to personality psychology* (4th ed.). New York: Wiley. p. 2.

McCrae, R.R., & Costa, P.T. (1987) Validation of the five-factor model of personality across instruments and observers. *Journal of Personality and Social Psychology*, 52, 81–90.

Motoyama, H. (1979). Yoga and oriental medicine. *Kundalini*, 3, 9–15.

Nagarathna, R. & Nagendra, H.R. (1980). Therapeutic Application of Yoga: a Report. Kanyakumari: Vivekananda Kendra Yoga Therapy and Research Centre.

Naudiyal S & Kumar K *Nada Yoga Evam Sangeet Sadhana Ka Manushya Ke Swasthya Par Padne Wale Prabhav Ka Addhyan; Shodh-Pragya,* Uttarakhand Sanskrit University, pp. 221–28.

Naug, R.N. (1975) Yoga therapy in neurotic disorders. *Indian Journal of Clinical Psychology*, 2, 87–90.

Negi A & Kumar K; A Study on the Effect of Yogic Intervention on R A Factor in Gout Patients; I*nternational Journal of Yoga and Allied Sciences*, Indian Association of Yoga, New Delhi Vol. 1, No. 2 Dec. 2012. pp. 126–130.

Newberg Andrew, et al. The measurement of regional cerebral blood flow during the complex cognitive task of meditation: A preliminary SPECT study. Psychiatry Resource. 2001; 106:113–122.

Norman, W. T. (1967). 2,800 personality trait descriptors: Normative operating characteristics for a university population. Department of Psychology, University of Michigan.

Okun, M.A. & Stock, W.A. (1984) Correlates and components of SWB. *Journal of Applied Genetology*, 61, 95–112.

Ornish, D. (1990). Reversing Heart Disease. New York: Ballantyne Books.

Pal A, Kumar K; Effect of Yogic Practices on lipid profile and body fat composition in patients of coronary artery disease; Complementary Therapies in Medicine (June 2011) 19, (3), pp. 122–127.

Pandya Dr. Pranav;(2005) Science and Spirituality – Awaken the Hidden Powers of Hearing by Nada Yoga Akhand Jyoti; Vol. 3, p. 23

Pandya P & Kumar K; Yoga Nidra & Its impact on Human Physiology; *Yoga Vijnan*, M.D.N.I.Y, New Delhi Vol. 1 Issue 1, (2007), pp. 1–8.

Patel, S. & Kumar, K. A study on the effect of Yoga and diet-control on Body mass index and cholesterol level of the Obese Youth *International Journal of Science and Consciousness*, Vol: 2, Issue 1 March 2016 pp. 13–17. ISSN:2455-2038

Paul, R. (1992, November). *Critical thinking defined.* Handout given at Critical Thinking Conference, Atlanta, GA. p. 9.

Paul, Richard (1992) Critical Thinking: What, Why and How. New Directions for Community Colleges, 77, 5–24

Pervin, L. A., Cervone, D., & John, O. P. (2005), *Personality: Theory and Research* (9th ed.) Hoboken, NJ: John Wiley & Sons. pp. 513.

Peter Salovey and John D. Mayer (1990) Emotional Intelligence, Imagination, Cognition and Personality 9 (3), pp. 185–211.

Pokhariyal K P & Kumar K; A study on the effect of Hatha Yogic Practices on Body weight of the Human subjects, ACADEMICIA, Volume 3, Issue 2, February, 2013, pp. 257–61.

Pokhriyal K P & Kumar K; Effect of Shatkarma practices on serum glucose and serum cholesterol level of the Human subjects: an Observation; *International Journal of Yoga and Allied Sciences*, Vol. 2, No. 1, 2013. pp. 10–13. ISSN: 2278-5159

Pt Shriram Sharma Acharya 1976 Dhyana Yoga Ka Vyavaharik Kriya Paksha, Yug Nirman Yojna Press, Mathura, p. 27.

Pt Shriram Sharma Acharya 2001 Music the Nector of Life, Gayatri Parivar Yug Nirman Yojna Trust, Maharastra, Andheri, Mumbai, p. 4

Rajvanshi, A.K., 2002 "Palliative Effect of Good Music", Editorial article in *Times of India*, April 15.

Ralph Linton (1936) The Study of Man: An Introduction, D. Appleton-Century Company, pp. 201–203.

Ramamurthi, B. (1977). Yoga and neurology. *Journal of Rehabilitation in Asia*, 18, 16–17.

Raymond Bernard Cattell (1957). Personality and motivation structure and measurement. New York, NY: World Book. pp. 124.

Robert E.Park and Ernest W. Burgess, Introduction to the Science of Sociology (Chicago, 1921), p. 55

Saraswati, Swami Karmananda (1982). Yoga averts heart attack. *Yoga*, 20, (5), 11–17.

Saraswati, Swami Muktananda (1982). Yoga nidra: Yoga, brain and consciousness. National Symposium conducted at NIMHANS, Bangalore.

Saraswati, Swami Niranjanananda (1993). Yoga Darshan, Sri Panchdashnam Paramahamsa Alakh Bara, Rikhia, Deoghar, Bihar.

Saraswati, Swami Niranjanananda (1996). The impact of yoga practices on jail inmates: A report from 24 jails in Bihar. (Unpublished paper), Bihar Yoga Bharati, Munger.

Saraswati, Swami Satyananda (1976). Four Chapters on Freedom, Bihar School of Yoga, Munger.

Saraswati, Swami Satyananda (1980). Yoga From Shore to Shore (3rd edition), Bihar School of Yoga, Munger.

Saraswati, Swami Satyananda (1981) Satsang and Psychotherapy, Yoga Magazine, Bihar School of Yoga, Munger July 1981, p. 6.

Saraswati, Swami Satyananda (1996). Asana Pranayama Mudra Bandha (New edition), Bihar Yoga Bharati, Munger.

Seithikurippu R. PandiPerumal, David Warren Spence, Neena Srivastava, Divya Kanchibhotla, Kamakhya Kumar, Gaurav Saurabh Sharma, Ravi Gupta & Gitanjali Batmanabane; The Origin and Clinical Relevance of Yoga Nidra; Sleep and Vigilance (2022) 6; pp. 61–84.

Sethi, B.B., Trivedi, J.K. & Anand, R. (1981). A comparative study of the relative effectiveness of biofeedback and shavasana in tension headache. *Indian Journal of Psychiatry*, 23, 109–114.

Sharma, I. and Agnihotri, S.S. (1982). Preliminary observations on the effect of controlled breathing in anxiety states. Yoga, brain and consciousness: National Symposium conducted at NIMHANS, Bangalore.

Shear MK, Greeno C, Kang J, et al (April 2000). "Diagnosis of nonpsychotic patients in community clinics". Am J Psychiatry 157 (4), 581–7.

Sheldon J Korchin (2004), *Modern Clinical Psychology,* New Delhi CBS, pp. 33- 34.

Shelvamurthy, W. (1996). The influence of yogic practices on Defence Scientists. *The Times of India*, Patna.

Silverman, DK (2005), "What Works in Psychotherapy and How Do We Know? What Evidence-Based Practice Has to Offer", *Psychoanalytic Psychology*, 22 (2):

Singh R K, & Kumar K; Achieving Human Excellence "The Yoga Way"; *International Journal of Yoga and Allied Sciences*, Vol. 10, No. 2, 2021, pp. 169–176.

Singh R K, Komal & Kumar K; Exploring Spiritual and Scientific dimensions of Om Chanting; *International Journal of Yoga and Allied Sciences*, Vol. 11, No. 2, 2022, pp. 95–102.

Singh, R.H., Shettiwar, R.M. & Udupa, K.N. (1978). The role of yogic practices in the prevention and treatment of hypertension. *Swasth Hind*, 22, 63–65.

Sixbenefitsofyogaformentalhealth(andhowtopractice).(n.d.)retrievedJune 16, 2024, from www.calm.com/blog/benefits-of-yoga-for-mental-health

Skinner B F.(1953) *Science and human behavior*. New York: Macmillan. p. 461

Smith G M (1967) Usefulness of peer rating of personality in Educational research. *Educational Psychological Measurement* (27), pp. 967–984

Steven K.H. Aung and Mathew H.M. Lee. Music, Sounds, Medicine, and Meditation: An Integrative Approach to the Healing Arts, *Alternative and Complementary Therapies*. October 2004, 10(5): 266–270

Strupp, H. & Binder, J. (1984): *Psychotherapy in a New Key, A Guide to Time-Limited Dynamic Psychotherapy*. Ed : Basic Books, Inc., Publishers, New York. p. 43.

Swami Bodhananda (1939) The Bhagavad Gita, Vedanta Society, p. 16

Swami Satyananda Saraswati (1982) Kirtan: Rocket to Self-realization, *Yoga Magazine*, Bihar School of Yoga, Munger Sept. 1982, p. 36.

Sysaro S, Occupational & Environmental Medicine, Vol. 60, 2003, pp. 3–9.

The Benefits of Yoga. (n.d.) retrieved June 16, 2024, from osteopathic.org

Udupa, K.N. "Stress and its management by yoga", Motilal Banarsidass Publication, pp. 305–320

Udupa, K.N., (1977). Pathogenesis and management of stress disorders. *Quart. J. Surg. Sci.*, Banaras Hindu University, 13(2): 56.

Uniyal A, Kumar K; Psychological approach of Yoga for Cancer Patients; *International Journal of Yoga and Allied Sciences*, Vol. 10, No. 1, 2021, pp. 31–35

Uniyal A, Kumar K; Yoga for Cancer Patients: A Review of the evidence-based researches; *Shodh-Pragya,* Uttarakhand Sanskrit University, Vol. 2020, No. 1. pp. 234–48.

Varma, L.P. (1979). Yoga, meditation and mysticism. *Indian Journal of Psychiatry*, 21, 293–304.

Verma S, Kumar K, & Meena R; Belief of Indian Population on Traditional Yoga System During COVID-19 Crisis; *Indian Journal of Traditional Knowledge*; N I S C A I R, New Delhi Vol. 19, No: 4 Oct 2020.

Verma S, Kumar K, & Meena R; Evidenced Based Study on General Wellbeing through Hatha Yoga; *International Journal of Science and Consciousness*, Vol. 3, Issue 4 Oct 2017, pp. 78–83.

Verma S, Kumar K, & Meena R; Impression of Group Consciousness on Alpha E.E.G. Brain Waves; *International Journal of Yoga and Allied Sciences*, Vol. 6, No. 1, 2017. pp. 37- 42.

Verma, S., Kashyap, G K., Kumar, K., Can Pranakarshan Pranayam helps to cope up with stress? *International Journal of Science and Consciousness*, Vol. 2, Issue 2 June 2016. pp. 38–45.

Verma, S., Kumar, K., Evidence-based comparative study of group and individual consciousness on life satisfaction among adults; *Yoga Mimansa*, Kaivalyadham, Lonavala, Maharastra Vol. 52 No. 1, 2020. pp. 34–37.

Verma, S., Kumar, K., Formulation of Yoga and Ayurveda; *International Journal of Science and Consciousness*, Vol. 4, No. 3, 2018, pp. 65–73.

Verma, S.K. (1988). Measurement of positive mental health: some theoretical and practical considerations. *Indian Journal of Clinical Psychology*, 15, 6–11.

Vrinte, Joseph (2002). *The perrnnial quest for a psychology with a soul.* Motilal Banarsidass Publishers.